HOW TO DO
just about
everything
to
SUCCEED

Courtney Rosen & the eHow Editors

TED SMART

This edition produced for The Book People Ltd, Hall Wood Avenue, Haydock, St Helens WA11 9UL

HarperCollins*Publishers*
Westerhill Road, Glasgow G64 2QT
www.collins.co.uk

This selection from *How To Do Just About Everything* first published by HarperCollins 2004

ISBN 0-00-772603-1

A catalogue record for this book is available from the British Library.

Printed and bound in Great Britain by Clays Ltd, St Ives plc
10 9 8 7 6 5 4 3 2 1

How To Do Just About Everything
Copyright © 2000, 2003 eHow, Inc. and Weldon Owen Inc.

UK Edition Produced by Grant Laing Partnership
Editors: Jane Simmonds, Helen Ridge and Terry Burrows
Designer: Christine Lacey

eHow, Inc.
Editor-in-Chief: William R. Marken
Book Editor: Sharon Rose Beaulaurier
Editors: Dale Conour, Julie Jares, Jason Jensen,
Roberta Kramer, Deborah McCaskey, Jill Metzler,
Sonya Mukherjee, Mimi Towle
Editorial Assistants: Shawn Asim, Linette Kim, Alison Goldberg, Matt Holohan
Creative Director: Patrick Barrett

Founder: Courtney Rosen
CFO: Mark Murray
VP of Engineering: Gladys Barnes
Director of Business Development: Jose Guerrero
General Counsel: James M. Hackett
VP of Commerce: Josh Prince
VP of Marketing: Kristen Sager
VP of Operations: Jeff Tinker
VP of Product Strategy: Joseph A. Vause
VP of Sales: Kevin Walsh

.com press
CEO: John Owen
President: Terry Newell
COO: Larry Partington
VP, International Sales: Stuart Laurence
VP, Publisher: Roger Shaw
Creative Director: Gaye Allen

Managing Editor: Janet Goldenberg
Art Director: Diane Dempsey
Series Manager: Brynn Breuner
Production & Layout: Joan Olson, Lorna Strutt
Production Director: Chris Hemesath

Project Coordinators: Margaret Garrou, Lorna Strutt
Contributing Edictors: Mandy Erickson, Norman Kolpas
Copy Chief: Elissa Rabellino
Copy Editors: Linda Bouchard, Claire Breen, Kathy Kaiser, Gail Nelson, Cynthia Rubin, David Sweet
Proofreader: Ruth Jacobson
Indexer: Ken DellaPenta

Courtney Rosen and other contributors to this book appear on behalf of eHow, Inc.

.com|press
.com press is a division of Weldon Owen Inc., 814 Montgomery Street, San Francisco, California 94133

CAREERS

College and Higher Learning

Job Search

Job Survival

FUN ACTIVITIES

Media and Celebrities

Entertainment, Literature and Art

Games and Skills

RELATIONSHIPS

Friendship and Dating

Wedding Bells

STYLE, ETIQUETTE AND PERSONAL CARE

HEALTH AND FITNESS

Self-Improvement

TRAVEL

Transport

Trip Preparation

Travel Tips

Destinations

SPORTS AND RECREATION

A Note to Readers

When attempting any of the described activities in this book, please note the following:

Risky activities Certain activities described in this book are inherently dangerous or risky. Before attempting any new activity, make sure you are aware of your own limitations and consider all applicable risks (whether listed or not).

Professional advice While we strive to provide complete and accurate information, it is not intended as a substitute for professional advice. You should always consult a professional whenever appropriate, or if you have any questions or concerns regarding medical, legal or financial advice.

Physical or health-related activities Be sure to consult your GP before attempting any health- or diet-related activity, or any activity involving physical exertion, particularly if you have any condition that could impair or limit your ability to engage in such an activity.

Adult supervision The activities described in this book are intended for adults only, and they should not be performed by children without responsible adult supervision.

Breaking the law The information provided in this book should not be used to break any applicable law or regulation.

All of the information in this book is obtained from sources that we believe are accurate and reliable. However, we make no warranty, express or implied, that the information is sufficient or appropriate for every individual, situation or purpose. Further, the information may become out of date over time. You assume the risk and full responsibility for all your actions, and eHow, Inc. and the publishers will not be liable for any loss or damage of any sort, whether consequential, incidental, special or otherwise, that may result from the information presented. The descriptions of third-party products and services in this book are for information only and are not intended as an endorsement by eHow, Inc. of any particular product or service.

Skill-level icons – ⟍ – indicate the ease or difficulty of each undertaking on a scale of one to five, with one being the easiest. In the last few pages you'll also find a keyword index to help you locate instructions for every task quickly.

Become a TV Presenter

The emergence of digital television has meant a proliferation of new cable and satellite channels. This means there are plenty of opportunities to be discovered for would-be TV presenters.

Steps

1. A fundamental requirement of a television presenter is the ability to project his or her personality in front of a camera. Although there is no substitute for real broadcast experience, domestic video equipment can help you to get used to being in the camera's gaze. Frequent video taping will also help you to assess your own performance.

2. What kind of TV presenter do you want to be? Someone fronting a music programme will usually have different skills to someone presenting a current affairs show. Watch a wide range of different programmes – on both terrestrial and cable/satellite – to see which areas interest you the most.

3. Are you an expert in anything? The chance to present a TV show often comes from fame in a specific field. Many sports presenters, for example, will previously have enjoyed successful sporting careers. As an expert in your field, send your CV to as many TV production companies, producers, researchers and media freelancers as you can.

4. Many successful presenters began life as TV journalists. Another common route is to work your way up within a TV production company – typically as a runner or researcher.

5. Which TV presenter would you choose as a role model? If someone already has your dream job, research how he or she got to that position. Try to identify what skills or qualities he or she possesses, and attempt to acquire them yourself. You might even try to contact him or her directly – you'll be surprised how many celebrities are flattered to be asked for their advice.

6. Plum jobs are rarely advertised: staff are often "head-hunted" or simply in the right place at the right time. Those with the best connections are usually first in line for the top positions.

Consider attending one of the many short courses available teaching simple techniques for on-camera behaviour. These are usually aimed at businessmen or executives who make periodic media appearances, but include lessons that any fledgling TV presenter will find useful.

⚠ Warning

Whatever a university prospectus may claim, a degree course in Media Studies or Broadcasting is unlikely – in itself – to lead to a job as a TV presenter.

2

Become a Vet

Although an eternally popular dream career for many young animal lovers, only students with the highest grades will have a chance of even getting an interview for vet school.

◉ Steps

1. By law, to work as a veterinary surgeon in the UK you must first be registered with the Royal College of Veterinary Surgeons (RCVS).

2. To join the RCVS you need a veterinary degree from one of the UK's six RCVS-approved vet schools. They are based at the universities of Bristol, Cambridge, Edinburgh, Glasgow, Liverpool and London.

3. This career is only open to the most academically able. Degree course entry qualifications are high – usually three grade-A A-levels. (Chemistry is mandatory; the other two subjects must include biology, physics or maths.)

4. Entrants will be expected to have gained practical experience of handling animals, usually at a veterinary practice.

5. Make sure you can finance your studies. Veterinary degrees take five years (six at Cambridge), and the nature of the study is such that taking a part-time job outside of college or during holidays won't be possible.

For every undergraduate place at vet school there are up to 20 applications. Since qualifications and work experience will be of a similar high standard, your acceptance may hinge on how well you perform at the entrance interview. It's therefore critical that you are well-prepared. Try to ask a recently qualified vet for tips on what to expect. Or get student views from a university vet school web page.

⚠ Warnings

You will often be on call during non-working hours, just like a medical doctor.

3

Become a Film Director

There are many paths to a career in directing films.

◉ Steps

1 Brainstorm to come up with any potential contacts in the film industry. Work as an apprentice under anyone currently directing student films, TV commercials, music videos or feature films.

2 Consider applying to film school to gain both knowledge and industry contacts.

3 Apply for work on film sets, in entry-level jobs such as production assistant – or as anyone's assistant. If you work hard and make friends, you can move up the ladder.

4 Target jobs directing TV commercials or music videos, where many film directors get their start.

5 Develop a reel (a tape of the work you've directed).

6 Make self-financed films of your own; to start with, they can be short (10 minutes long) and shot on easily accessible and affordable DV video equipment. If necessary, cast and write your films yourself to build your experience and CV.

7 Send postcards and updates regularly to industry contacts you have made, including directors, producers and actors. Constant networking leads to opportunities.

Dream Jobs

Be creative and persistent, and understand that there isn't one right way to become a film director.

Read *The Hollywood Reporter* and *Variety* to find out about upcoming productions and possible job openings.

Network, network, network.

⚠ Warning

As with most jobs in the field of entertainment, directors work long and irregular hours.

4

Become a Photographer

To be successful in this satisfying career, you need an artistic eye, technical skills, a knack for marketing yourself and a passion for your work.

⊙ Steps

1. Take pictures for your school magazine or student newspaper after you have studied the basics. You will get an idea of how deep your passion is for the medium.

2. Decide which type of photography – such as news, advertising or fine-art photography – best suits your interests and talents.

3. A degree in photography may help you get your foot in the door of some more prestigious employers. In general, though, practical experience is far more marketable than any academic achievement.

4. Develop an outstanding portfolio. Include excellent photographs you have taken on your own – in particular, those focusing on your own specialised themes.

5. Be willing to work as a photographer's assistant once you have some experience. You are unlikely to be competing with experienced photographers for a while.

6. Realise that more than half of all photographers work on a freelance

basis. Many magazines and organisations that use photographers do not employ them directly.

7 Attend workshops and seminars to remain up-to-date about new technical advances in photography.

 Tips

Use the best camera equipment you can afford.

Take classes in business and public relations if you eventually want to set up your own studio.

Volunteer your services as an assistant to a local studio photographer. It's good on-the-job training and may result in a full-time position.

Consider using stock photo agencies to sell your photos.

⚠ Warning

If you become a photojournalist you must be willing to travel at a moment's notice, and also be prepared to work irregular hours.

5

Become an Interior Designer

Professionals in this field design and furnish the interiors of commercial, industrial and residential buildings. They have to combine artistic flourish with a working knowledge of statutory building regulations.

Steps

1 Understand that as an interior designer you will need to know more than how to decorate a space. For example, you will need to fully understand building regulations, be able to easily read a blueprint and know how to communicate with engineers, architects and clients.

2 Unlike the fields of architecture or medicine, there is no legislation or industry body which requires qualified membership as a necessity to work. But although anyone could theoretically set up as an interior designer, most working in the field have some sort higher education – HND or BA degree – most commonly from an art school.

3 When choosing a design course at art school or university, make sure that it includes a module on computer-aided design (CAD). As a

modern designer you will be expected to know how to use a computer to create either two- or three-dimensional designs.

4   Some interior design degree courses incorporate periods of industrial placement, which give students the opportunity to obtain genuine work experience in a design or architecture practice – if, usually, in a low-paid junior capacity. Following graduation, students with practical experience are generally the most sought-after – some are even offered full-time jobs with their placement employers.

5   Most experienced interior designers working in Britain operate either within small business partnerships or freelance. With less security than those in full-time employment, this lifestyle is not to everyone's liking.

 Tip

Subscribe to interior design and architecture magazines to learn about the latest trends.

 Warning

Designers often work irregular hours, at the convenience of their clients.

6

Become a Private Detective

Private detectives are used by lawyers and solicitors, insurance companies, businesses and individual members of the public. They are usually self-employed.

Steps

1   Forget the mysterious world-weary characters from Raymond Chandler novels: most people working as private detectives are experienced professionals from a military or law enforcement background.

2   If you don't have an investigative background you may need to acquire certain skills to help with your work, such as learning how to fingerprint, conduct an interview, take samples of evidence or write reports.

3   Polish your writing skills. This is one of the most important things you

can do to ensure success. You'll need to write reports frequently, and they must be of professional quality.

4   Become proficient at using credit checks and computer searching resources.

5   You do not need any form of government licence to operate as a private detective. However you may reach a wider client base if you are a member of the Association of British Investigators (10 Bonner Hill Road, Kingston Upon Thames, Surrey, KT1 3EP), or the Institute of Professional Investigators, Burnhill Business Centre, provident House, Burrell Row, High Street, Beckenham, Kent, BR3 1AT.

 Tips

Honestly assess how well equipped you are for such a career. You need to be mature, assertive, persistent and logical.

⚠ Warning

Be prepared for long, irregular, solitary work hours, especially during surveillance work.

If it's the "glamour" of the TV and cinema private eye that attracts you to this career, think again. Most of your time will be spent in fairly mundane pursuits such as checking out credit ratings. And while it may not be a job for the faint-hearted, British gun legislation means that it's unlikely that you'll ever find yourself in the middle of a shoot-out.

7

Become a Chef

A chef is a highly skilled and inventive cook who can turn a delicious meal into an artistic presentation. It usually takes years to become accomplished and known in this field.

◉ Steps

1   Work in a restaurant for the experience, even if it is in a non-cooking position. You will learn what it is like to be on your feet for long hours.

2   Find out if there is a local catering college, or suitable college/university courses in your area.

3   Decide what type of cooking you would like to do and in what type of kitchen you would like to work.

4   Although dedicated college courses will teach you valuable skills, it is more likely to be practical experience in a commercial environment that impresses potential employers.

5   Be aware that an apprenticeship will almost certainly require you to work at first in the least-skilled jobs in the kitchen. As you develop, you can advance up the culinary ladder in a larger restaurant by becoming a line chef, sous-chef, head chef, executive chef and, finally, master chef. Pastry chefs follow their own distinct ladder.

6   The restaurant business in the UK is more conscious of trends in food than in most other countries, with influence usually coming from the hippest of London's eating establishments. A poorly paid apprenticeship served at a Michelin-rated restaurant is a path trodden by many of today's most noted celebrity chefs.

7   If you think you would like to open your own restaurant, take a business course that specialises in catering. Look for one that places equal emphasis on health and safety legislation and aspects of business finance – getting a loan, hiring staff, dealing with taxation, pension and national insurance issues.

❄ Tips

Be certain that this is the career to which you want to devote your time. Initially, consider taking a short course at a catering college while working in a restaurant kitchen.

Stay up-to-date on food trends and kitchen equipment. Read as many culinary magazines and journals as possible.

Choose an area of specialisation if you want to work in up-market restaurants.

⚠ Warning

If the head chef leaves, his or her entire staff may be asked to (or choose to) do the same.

8

Become a Radio Disc Jockey

You need confidence, a pleasant speaking voice and excellent communication skills for this job. On the air, you may introduce music, conduct interviews, and read commercials or even the news and weather forecast.

⊙ Steps

1 Take public speaking and drama courses at school or university. Make tapes of your speaking voice and ask your speech and drama teachers for their opinion of your vocal projection.

2 Consider taking any relevant part-time unpaid work. Working as a mobile disc jockey at friends' parties will also provide useful experience – especially if you have the opportunity to work with an experienced professional.

3 Find out about those colleges and universities that offer an education in broadcasting.

4 Be aware, however, that although many universities now offer degrees in broadcasting, this may not be the best way to a broadcasting career. For example, the majority of successful "talking heads" in the areas of news and current affairs are more likely to have crossed over from a background in political journalism.

5 If you are a student, help with your college radio station by doing any work that will teach you about the practical side of radio broadcasting, a station's equipment and the problems associated with airtime. Offer to be the DJ or radio announcer at the station during unusual hours. Then make a tape of the show and include the experience on your CV.

6 Try to get part-time work in local radio or as hospital radio volunteer. At first you will more than likely be doing dull office work rather than talking into a microphone or running the board. But the experience will be valuable.

7 If the opportunity presents itself, consider a job in local radio after you have completed your education. You're almost certain to begin with an entry-level position aimed at showing you the ropes, but – if you're ambitious – your chances of getting airtime in the near future will be

far greater than on a larger station. Most national radio positions will require you to have had several years of on-air experience.

 Tips

Become an expert on a variety of interesting topics. Prepare a demo CD that demonstrate your knowledge and your excellent speaking voice.

Time management during a show and the ability to connect with your audience are key skills to have in this field.

⚠ Warning

Be prepared for the possibility of unusual working hours if you become a DJ.

9
Become a Model

With supermodel salaries matching those of pop stars, it's no surprise that so many are attracted to a career in modelling.

⊙ Steps

1. Be aware that only the tiniest percentage of wannabe models actually succeed. If you are rejected it WILL be for reasons that may be deeply hurtful to you.

2. To work as a model you need representation by an agency. You won't even get a look-in if you fail to meet certain physical criteria. For a woman, you must be: at least 1.7 m (5 ft 7 in) tall; 81–89-cm (32–35-in) bust; 56–64-cm (22-25-in) waist; 84–91-cm (33-36-in) hips; clear skin; healthy hair; immaculately straight white teeth. Male models need to be at least 1.8 m (6 ft) tall.

3. Many of the household names were "discovered" by agencies in very ordinary settings. They can spot potential – however well masked – walking down any high street. Some of the most famous models didn't even have ambitions in this area until approached by an agency.

4. If you are trying to get your first break you need some photographs. Get as many pictures taken as possible, and then choose the best five images to be blown up to 25 x 20 cm (10 x 8 in) format. Have three sets made: mount the first on black A4 card and slot them in an A4 display folder (this is the start of your portfolio); keep the second set

safe, along with the negatives; keep the third set to send to your first agency contact.

5   Get a list of modelling agencies: go to a public library and look in the Yellow Pages – the vast majority of major modelling agencies will be based in the Central London area.

6   Telephone your target agencies. Tell them you have some photographs and would like to get some opinions of your potential.

7   If asked for photographs, send them in a hard-backed envelope, along with a typed covering letter detailing your measurements. If you haven't heard anything in seven days, call again to check that your pack arrived safely. If the agency shows no interest, get another set of prints made and contact another agency.

8   Don't be disheartened by a few rejections. If, however, a dozen or more agencies turn you down, then you must assume that you just don't have the look they are currently after.

❋ Tips

Have your portfolio photographs shot on a white background. Include some close-ups of your head and shoulders (both with and without makeup). Take a mixture of colour and black and white images. Include some swimwear shots – although avoid anything that even vaguely resembles soft porn.

⚠ Warning

There is no point in using your photographs to hide physical shortcomings. These will become apparent as soon as you meet agency staff, and will only waste everyone's time.

10

Become a Celebrity

What makes a celebrity? Something indefinable that makes us mere mortals think beyond a person's ability, to want to know every last detail of their lives.

◎ Steps

1   An obvious starting point for most is to become exceptionally good or successful in a sphere of work. But that's not the only way.

2   If you have no discernible talent, an alternative is to appear on a "Reality TV" show, such as *Big Brother*. Beware, however, that celebrity without the talent to back it up is usually short-lived.

3   Behave in a way that keeps your name on the front pages of the tabloid newspapers. A romantic liaison with another celebrity is usually a good guarantee of coverage.

4   Hire public relations staff – their job is to keep you in the headlines. (You'll need a seven-figure bank account if you want to engage a top PR company for any length of time.)

5   Invite celebrity magazines such as *OK* and *Hello* to photograph you and your loved ones in the glamorous surroundings of your home.

6   Appear on as many chat shows as you can. If the opportunity arises, do something shocking that will get reported in the following day's press.

7   Make sure you know – and can get into – the hippest joints in town. Make sure there is someone there to photograph you as you enter and when you leave – preferably arm-in-arm with another celebrity.

✷ Tip

Hire a society party planner to organise your gatherings. They will be able to guarantee a high celebrity count in attendance … for a fee, of course.

11

Become Prime Minister

There is no standard career path to holding the highest-profile job in Britain. But somebody's got to do it, so why not you?

◉ Steps

1   The prime minister is the leader of a democratically elected political party. As politics since World War II has been dominated by three parties, that means first becoming leader of the Labour party, Conservative party or Liberal Democrats (although the latter has not yet managed to provide a premier).

2. Before you become party leader you must be an elected member of parliament. You are also likely to have first served as a cabinet minister (or shadow cabinet minister).

3. To become an MP you must be chosen to represent your party at a parliamentary election. Most MPs will have participated in politics from their teenage years – often in the youth wings of their parties – and become party activists concurrent with their studies and subsequent careers.

4. Most MPs switch from a different career once they have been elected to parliament. The combative oratory nature of parliamentary politics means that some of the most successful politicians were once lawyers.

❋ Tips

Many successful parliamentary MPs have started in politics as local government councillors. The Trades Union movement has also provided a number of leading politicians.

Get Rich

It's easy to make a fortune: deal in stocks and shares, start your own internet company, win the lottery. Right? Wrong. To even be in with a chance of getting rich requires clear thinking.

Steps

1. Decide what "rich" means to you. Does it mean money for everything you need? Money for everything you want? Enough to retire where you live now? Enough to retire and live in the South of France?

2. Start saving. Most experts agree that investing 10 to 15 per cent of your gross monthly income will create a comfortable nest egg for later years.

3. Take advantage of compound interest – earning interest on your interest by letting investment returns accumulate and build on themselves.

4. Be conscious of cost. For example, if you buy a second-hand car instead of a new one, and invest the balance, you will have thousands of pounds more when you retire.

5. Take care of yourself. This will reduce medical costs later on in life, as well as extend the years you can work – and save.

6. A better education is more likely to result in high earnings. Some studies have shown that graduates are likely to earn an average annual salary of £15,000 more than those with no higher education. The gap is even higher for holders of a postgraduate degree.

7. Get married. Married people are generally healthier than single people. Plus, they can economise on expenses, and they have more to invest. And because married people live longer, they can work and save longer.

8. Enjoy yourself. Don't be so concerned with amassing a fortune that you neglect to enjoy life now. Strive for balance.

Use a planning calculator (you'll find these on many personal finance web pages) to work out how much you need to save each year to achieve a specific goal.

Little expenses add up. Switch to regular coffee each morning, rather than a double-shot latte, put the pound you save in a fund, and you could have up to £50,000 more at retirement.

Work out how much you'll need to maintain your current lifestyle. Ask a financial adviser for help if you need it.

⚠ Warning

Don't waste the money you do have on "get-rich-quick" schemes, lotteries or gambling.

13

Create an Investment Portfolio

A high-performing portfolio is every investor's goal. First, you'll need to develop your own objectives and strategies.

◉ Steps

1. Determine what items or events you're saving for. These can be retirement, a new home, your children's education or anything else you choose.

2. Determine when you want to retire, purchase your home or send your children to college, to help you decide what percentage return you need to earn on your initial investment.

3. Decide how much money to invest. Invest what you can comfortably afford now, keeping in mind that you can change that amount later.

4. Determine how much risk you are willing to take. Some investments that generate high returns may be riskier than others.

5. Once you decide the amount you are willing to invest, the returns you want to achieve, when you need the money and how much risk you are willing to accept, put together your investment portfolio.

6   Talk to a financial advisor or stockbroker. Tell them your objectives and ask them to suggest ways in which you can allocate your money. (Be aware that there is a fee for this kind of service, though.)

7   Re-evaluate your portfolio at least annually. Analyse each investment.

✳ Tips

With less than £20,000 to invest, consider managed funds rather than individual shares to diversify and balance risk.

Tax-free government bonds usually generate lower returns, but they also pose less of a risk.

⚠ Warning

Allocate only a portion of your savings to stocks and shares, depending on your age and tolerance for risk. Invest the balance in other approaches, such as cash ISAs, pension plans or bonds.

14

Make Good Investments

Whether you are a first-time investor or an investment guru, mistakes happen. The key to avoiding mishaps is to keep on top of investment rules, tax codes and annual reports.

◎ Steps

1   Study. Read financial news, personal-finance magazines, corporate annual and quarterly reports, registration statements and prospectuses for the financial products you're considering.

2   Develop goals and strategies to meet your goals. Use these to choose shares and other investments. Ask for professional advice if you are uncomfortable investing on your own.

3   Diversify. Avoid putting large portions of your portfolio in a single stock or industry so that you're not so affected by its movements.

4   Take advantage of tax concessions by investing in ISAs or Stakeholder pensions.

5   Buy shares that you plan to keep for three to five years. Remember that

"good" shares at unrealistically high prices are a bad buy. Aim to buy at a low price, sell at a high price (see 16 "Research Shares to Buy").

6 Invest in what you know, and avoid buying shares in unfamiliar industries and companies.

7 Shop for total value. That means learning to calculate key statistics, such as price-earnings ratios, so you can compare shares.

8 Resist fads. If everyone is buying gold, variable annuities or some other investment, watch out. The herd soon will change direction – look what eventually happened to the internet company boom of the late 1990s.

9 Know when to sell. Your objective may be to hold particular shares or mutual funds for three to five years, but if its track record looks like terminal descent, bail out.

Things You'll Need

- ☐ financial newspapers and magazines
- ☐ corporate reports
- ☐ relevant prospectuses

15

Understand the Stock Market

Before you take the plunge, here are some key steps to consider towards building an understanding of the stock market.

◉ Steps

1 Understand "equity securities". As an investor, when you buy shares you take an ownership stake in a company and assume a corresponding degree of risk – so you could end up losing all of your money.

2 Learn the language of the market, familiarising yourself with such financial terms as "price-earnings [PE] ratio", "margin", "option", "earnings per share" and "leverage".

Personal Finance

3   Analyse the holdings of a number of successful fund companies, noting which shares they have held – and those discarded – over the past three or four years.

4   Make a habit of reading the quarterly and annual reports filed by the biggest players on the FTSE 100 index.

5   Research companies of which you have personal knowledge – and a high degree of confidence. Evaluate their financial reporting, looking for trends that indicate growth and continuing profitability.

6   Get online. Dozens of companies offer financial news, advice and analysis online (see 16 "Research Shares to Buy").

7   Take advantage of all the information your stockbroker has to offer regarding individual shares. Always know what you are buying – and why – before you invest.

8   Invest on paper for a few weeks and carefully monitor the performance of your prospective portfolio before you actually apply to buy stocks and shares.

 ## Tips

Invest in reputable companies and stick with them for the long haul.

When paying for financial advice, make sure that you know the brokerage fees beforehand. These can vary to a surprising degree.

Set up an electronic portfolio of your stocks through an online service such as Yahoo! Finance. This will allow you to monitor your shares' performance throughout the day and to get the latest news about the companies you've invested in (see 18 "Monitor Shares").

If you don't have the time to do your own research, invest in a managed fund that has had good returns for at least three years.

⚠ Warning

Be prepared for a roller-coaster ride. The market can be volatile.

Research Shares to Buy

One of the most important parts of "playing the market" is researching companies.

◎ Steps

1 Obtain quarterly and annual corporate financial statements. You can get such documents without charge from a number of sources, among them, Company Annual Reporting Online (www.carol.co.uk).

2 Analyse quarterly statements covering two or three years, noting trends in earnings per share and revenue.

3 Look for a trend of consistent growth in earnings per share.

4 Calculate the company's price-earnings (PE) ratio, a measure of a stock's value. (Divide the stock price by annual earnings per share.)

5 Compare the PE ratio with industry norms. The lower the ratio, the less expensive the stock is relative to earnings.

6 Beware of debt. Check out the company's balance sheet, looking for the extent of its long-term debt.

7 Check cashflow – the movement of cash through the company. You'll want the company to have positive cashflow.

✹ Tips

Make sure the company doesn't ignore research and development – this may have implications for the future.

Calculate a sales-per-employee figure and compare the company with its competitors.

Assess the board. Use corporate reporting to discover where directors worked before they joined the company.

Buy Shares

Buying shares in a company is relatively easy once you've researched the companies you're interested in and have a broker or brokerage account to handle your purchase.

Steps

1. Educate yourself fully about shares before purchasing them. You can find information about shares and brokers on the internet.

2. Determine what you want in a broker or brokerage account. Do you want to meet with someone face-to-face? Will you want to be able to reach someone by phone? Do you require internet access? Is price your only consideration? Do you want to buy and sell only shares, or would you also like to buy and sell mutual funds, bonds or foreign stocks?

3. Choose a broker or brokerage firm to purchase the shares on your behalf based on your needs. If you need a lot of advice, begin with a full-service brokerage: the less expensive brokers may not offer advice. If you are fairly confident and want low prices, go for an online broker.

4. Contact a broker or firm and request an application. Many firms offer online applications, although most require that you send a payment to actually open the account.

5. Deliver a cheque in person if possible to speed up the process.

6. Begin buying and selling shares once your account is open.

7. Review the statements you receive and re-evaluate your portfolio's performance. Are you moving towards your investment goals?

Tips

Ask friends and colleagues for recommended stockbrokers. If you don't have a personal recommendation, read adverts in investment magazines, or such publications as the *Financial Times*.

An online broker is convenient and fast but can be susceptible to computer glitches. Ask if you will be able to make trades by telephone if ever necessary.

18

Monitor Shares

Monitoring the rising and falling prices of shares is an essential part of being a successful investor or shares trader.

⊙ **Steps**

1 Monitor the price of your shares on a daily basis, noting whether they are heading up, down or fluctuating. You can find your shares in the broadsheet newspapers or on the internet.

2 Track performance by reading monthly statements from your broker. Use the internet for up-to-the-minute tracking when needed. (You can create a portfolio of shares on your personalised home page.)

3 Closely monitor the shares you are interested in (not just those you own, but those you might buy). Monitoring can help you make an immediate decision on whether to buy, sell or hold.

4 Add to shares you like or those that are growing nicely when you have additional income to invest. Remember to diversify your investments.

5 Contact your broker by phone or the internet to buy or sell shares.

6 Specify the action you want to take and at what price you want to take it. Your broker will do the rest and provide you with a confirmation of your transaction when your order is executed.

 Tips

The stock market can be extremely volatile. It is advisable to keep a three-year horizon in mind. Day trading can be very profitable, but requires a high degree of knowledge as well as constant attention.

Read the *Financial Times* and read or watch any daily news that informs you about your shares and events that affect the stock market.

A share's performance should be compared with that of others in its group and evaluated over time – don't automatically sell your shares if you notice that they are declining in price.

19
Trade Online

Online trading depends on the same principles and skills as off-line trading, so use them to guide your thinking and actions.

Steps

1. Have a long, serious and brutally honest talk with yourself (and perhaps a trusted friend) about the kind of personality you have – you'll need to be disciplined and goal-orientated if you are to succeed.

2. Be sure you have at least £3,000 in easily available funds.

3. Set limits to your trading activity, such as number of transactions and/or commission paid, for an initial three-month period.

4. Research at least three online brokerage services and read all the "terms and conditions" statements concerning trading accounts.

5. Open an account with the brokerage service you choose for the minimum amount necessary to trade.

6. Write down all your trading (buys and sells) immediately after they have been executed: date, time, quantity and price per share of the actual purchase. Use these records for tax preparation and save them in case you are audited.

7. Evaluate your performance at the end of the three months. What were your gains and losses? Emotional reaction to the process? Did you stick to your goals?

Tip

Free research online is available from many of the big investment firms. Avoid fee-for-service features of your account unless they will directly improve your ability to trade intelligently.

Warnings
All laws regarding securities trading apply to trading online.

Technical service calls and broker advice over the phone are rarely free – check first.

Never trade on advice from chat rooms, message boards or any other questionable sources.

Trade only with your savings until you are experienced. Only then consider borrowing to trade.

20

Invest for Your Child's Future

Using money you can put aside regularly, and your child's own contributions from allowances and birthday funds, you can create a tidy nest egg for your child's future.

⊙ Steps

1   Start early and let compound interest work in your favour. If you can afford it, start paying into a stakeholder pension from birth. You can pay in up to £2,808 per year and the government will top that up to £3,600. Even if you can only afford £10 per month, it will give your child a useful springboard from which they can eventually make their own regular contributions.

2   Be aware that any investment you make that involves stocks and shares could go down in value. As always, take a long-term view when investing in the stock market. Although performance has been poor in recent times, the overall picture has remained upwardly mobile for the past century.

3   When setting up a college fund, try to make the best estimate you can of the figures you wish to achieve by the time your child reaches student age. If the cost of a three-year degree course is presently around £30,000 (in living expenses and fees) it could be more than double that figure in 18 years' time.

4   Even if you invest a small monthly amount in a modest "safe" building society, the compound interest will accrue impressively over the years.

5   Monitor your funds carefully to ensure that they are on track to meet your needs. If, for example, your 13-year-old daughter announces that she wants to become a doctor you'll need to increase your contributions accordingly to cover the cost of training.

Personal Finance

Ask relatives who regularly send cash gifts to consider putting that money into a savings account for your child.

Teach the significance of finance from an early age. Try to give your children a say in how money is invested on their behalf. Let your children see the benefits of making their own contributions to their funds – how, say, contributing a proportion of their weekly allowance or part-time earnings could mean the difference between their having to work through college and having the time to devote to study and leisure.

21

Live Within Your Budget

Living within your budget can be challenging. A few simple practices can help ensure that you are successful.

⊙ Steps

1   List all of your expenses, savings and income from the past year. Use your bank statement, credit card receipts and bills to do this. There are many computer-based financial programs that may help.

2   Determine, as accurately as possible, what expenses you expect to have over the next year. You can project expenses for a shorter period, such as the next three months, then multiply by four for yearly expenses.

3   Enter this information into a ledger or computer program (home finance software or as spreadsheet) to accurately track income and expenses.

4   Determine what you can reasonably afford to spend each month and then track how well you are doing by entering actual expenses into the ledger or computer program.

5   If you find that you are spending less than you had anticipated, you may want to put more money in your savings account to help out with unexpected expenses.

6   If you find that you are spending more than anticipated, try identifying the items you don't necessarily need (new clothes, CDs, eating out) and avoid purchasing them until you are back within your budget.

Allocate a portion of your income for savings and retirement – for example, company, personal or stakeholder pension plans.

Consider setting aside up to 20 per cent of your take-home income for savings.

⚠️ Warning

Avoid trying to forecast your expenses too far into the future. Doing so can result in inaccurate budgets and overspending.

22

Calculate Your Net Worth

Calculating your net worth is easy if the necessary information is readily available. Doing this will help you when deciding whether to make major purchases.

◎ Steps

1   List all of your fixed assets, such as property and cars, at their current value.

2   List all of your liquid assets: cash, bank accounts, shares and bonds.

3   List all jewellery, furniture and household items at their current value.

4   Add together all of the above. These are your total assets.

5   Subtract all of your debts, such as your mortgage, car loan and credit card balances, from your total assets. The result is your net worth.

6   Re-evaluate and update your net worth calculations on an annual basis.

Tips

Be realistic when evaluating the current value of your assets. Such information can be useful in determining whether you are adequately insured. Share the information with your insurance company to help you decide.

Remember to use the net value (after-tax) of any stocks, shares and bonds when calculating their value.

Calculate Your Credit Standing

Lenders use your debt-to-income ratio – or how much you owe on credit cards and loans compared with how much you earn – to help evaluate your credit standing.

Steps

1. Add up your total net monthly income. This includes your monthly wages and any overtime, commissions or bonuses that are guaranteed; plus any other payments received, such as interest or maintenance payment. If your income varies, calculate the monthly average for the past two years. Include any additional income.

2. Add up your monthly debt obligations. This includes all of your credit card bills, loan and mortgage payments. Make sure to include your monthly rent payments if applicable.

3. Divide your total monthly debt obligations by your total monthly income. This is your total debt-to-income ratio.

4. If your ratio is higher than 0.36 – which industry professionals would call a score of 36 – you need to take action. The lower the score, the better. A figure higher than 36 places you in danger of credit refusal, or may result in a higher interest rate.

Tip

When you tally your total monthly debts, use the minimum payment on your statements.

Warning

Unreported earned income cannot be used in the calculation.

24

Establish Credit

Credit isn't established overnight. Prepare yourself for
financial emergencies by securing a good credit rating.

Steps

1. Get current and savings accounts in your own name.

2. Apply for a credit card or charge card in your own name from a retail
store or financial institution. Make at least a minimum payment
monthly to establish a record of managing debt.

3. Apply for a loan in your name to buy jewellery, furniture or another
item that will be paid off in instalments for at least a year. Make all
payments on time.

4. Secure a small loan from a finance company or bank and make sure
that you pay instalments on time.

5. Check your credit rating by calling your creditors or ordering a copy of
your credit report.

6. If you experience trouble getting a loan, ask a friend or family member
to guarantee it.

Tips

Although not a credit indicator, a current or savings account shows how
you manage money. Avoid bouncing cheques and add to your savings
monthly.

The death of a spouse or a divorce could leave you without credit.
Always establish credit in your own name.

Secure a job for several months before applying for credit.

25

Get Out of Debt

Getting out of debt is challenging, but it can be accomplished
with dedication and perseverance.

Personal Finance

1 Cut up your credit cards except for one or two to use for emergencies. Throw away the pieces.

2 Contact lenders and request a lower interest rate on your debt.

3 Transfer as much debt as possible to the credit card that has the lowest interest rate, or get a debt-consolidation loan from a bank at a lower rate.

4 Use cash for all your purchases, and only buy what you can afford.

5 Commit to start paying off your debts one at a time and do it. Pay off the credit card and loans with the highest interest rate first.

6 Double your payments on the next debt by taking the payment you made on the first debt and adding it to the current debt.

7 Triple your payments on the next debt by combining payment amounts. Continue until all your credit cards and other debts are paid off.

✽ Tips

If you are a property owner, consider extending your mortgage to pay off other debts. (Do this only if your mortgage rate is lower than the interest rate you are paying elsewhere.)

Use consumer credit agencies to arrange repayment of debt. Many are free.

26

Find a Flat to Rent

Finding the right flat – in the right price range, with the right amenities, in the right area of town – isn't hard if you know how to manage the process. Here's what to do.

⊙ Steps

1 Work out how much you can afford. Be sure to include utilities.

2 Think carefully about where you'd like to live. Consider commuting times to your workplace and the types of amenities you'd like your local neighbourhood to offer.

3 Write down what features are important to you, such as parking, security, proximity to public transportation, laundry facilities, acceptable pet policies, and number of bedrooms and bathrooms.

4 Scan the "flats to let" listings in the local newspaper where you want to live; ask friends and work colleagues to keep an eye out for vacancies; check online services; look for adverts in corner shops.

5 Keep a file of newspaper adverts, computer printouts and notes. Go through your file and call for appointments to see your choice. Make note of any additional information you get.

6 Sign up with an agency service if you are new to the area, can't get around, don't have time to go through the classifieds or want fewer choices to consider.

7 Inspect flats carefully.

8 Agree terms with the landlord – most will require a deposit of one month's rent.

9 Establish a move-in date, sign a contract and arrange to pay the deposit and rent required.

✳ Tips

Drive past prospective buildings to get a feel for the neighbourhood.

The internet can provide useful information on prospective areas.

⚠ Warning

Flat-finding agencies often get commissions from landlords, so beware of any service that demands a hefty fee from prospective tenants.

27

Assert your Rights as a Tenant

You may not be the owner of the property in which you are living, but the law affords you certain rights as a lease-holding rent payer.

◉ Steps

1 If your landlord violates the lease, then he is in breach of contract.

2   If you are experiencing difficulties with your landlord it is important to get advice quickly. Greater problems can often arise if you don't take action at the right time. Keep copies of any letters you write and a note of any phone calls you make, including the time and date.

3   As a tenant, you have the exclusive rights to live in a property while your lease is valid – the landlord cannot move someone else in.

4   If you pay a deposit on the property before you move in, you should be given a receipt. You should get the full deposit back when you leave as long as there is no damage to the property under the agreement. If you pay weekly rent you must be issued with a rent book which shows your payments and is signed by the landlord.

5   Your landlord cannot enter the property without your permission or stop you having overnight guests. You should let in the landlord to do repairs but he or she should give you 24 hours' notice except in an emergency.

6   Get advice quickly if your landlord tries to change the locks, cut off gas, electricity or water, interfere with your post, or harass you. This is illegal. Contact your local Citizen's Advice Bureau (www.citizensadvice.org.uk) for help.

7   Landlords are responsible for most major repairs in rented property, such as roofing, garden fences, guttering, central heating and gas boilers. By law they must have the gas system checked every year by a registered CORGI (Council for Registered Gas Installers) engineer.

✹ Tips

The landlord is not necessarily the enemy. Do not jump to conclusions if your landlord is being unresponsive to your attempts at communication.

Here are some web pages that may be useful to renters:

Commission for Racial Equality (cre.gov.uk); Council for Registered Gas Installers (corgi-gas.com); Homeless Link (homeless.org.uk); Local Government Ombudsmen (lgo.org.uk/index.htm); The Housing Corporation (housing.org.uk); Tenant Participation Advisory Service (TPAS) (tpas.org.uk)

⚠ Warning

You cannot legally become a tenant in a property until you are 18 years old. If you are under 18 you may only be able to live in rented accommodation as a licensee.

Buy a House

You'll do a lot of house-hunting, deal with estate agents and building societies – and then hope the seller accepts your offer.

⊙ Steps

1 Work out how much you can afford to pay for your new house. Consider your deposit, stamp duty, estate agent's fee, mortgage, and buildings and contents insurance.

2 Decide where you want to live. Think about how long it will take to commute to work, local schools, and the re-sale value of the houses in the area.

3 Think about what kind of house you want. Do you want a newer house that requires little or no refurbishing? Would you prefer an older house with character that might require some repair work? One floor or two? Are you interested in a flat, terrace, semi-detached or townhouse?

4 Register with an estate agent. Have the details of properties that fall within your brief sent to you. Visit any properties that interest you: the more houses you look at, the better idea you will have of your likes and dislikes. This will help you filter out future choices.

5 You don't have to buy through an estate agent. Many people prefer to sell privately, advertising in newspapers or magazines.

6 Find a lender – usually an bank or a building society – and arrange to have pre-approval for a mortgage. A dedicated mortgage broker may be able to find a deal more suited to your needs – but you will be charged for the service.

7 Find your ideal house and make an offer.

8 Any mortgage lender will insist that you have the prospective property surveyed. (If you are paying the full quantity in cash you should still have the property surveyed.)

9 Hire a solicitor specialising in buying and selling property. They will perform the necessary searches to prove that the property is registered in the name of the vendor. If you choose not to hire a

solicitor you must do this for yourself – although possible, it is also time-consuming and arguably not worth the money you'll save.

10 Agree a date on which you can take possession of the property.

11 Once your solicitor has exchanged contracts with the vendor you can move in.

Be patient. Finding a house that fits your family's needs can take some time.

House values fluctuate with the ups and downs of the economy.

Buying a house is likely to be the biggest single investment you'll ever make. Choose wisely.

29

Determine How Big a Mortgage You Can Afford

Before you look for that dream house, you need to ask yourself what you can really afford to spend each month. And how much a mortgage lender is prepared to lend.

◉ Steps

1 Before you begin house hunting, consult a building society, bank or mortgage broker to find out the maximum loan you are likely have at your disposal.

2 Be aware that the amount you are allowed to borrow will vary from lender to lender. This will depend on your personal circumstances, such as regular income or assets. A typical figure for the UK would be up to four times a single annual income (although multiples of six have been known in recent years) or 80 per cent of the value of any owned property you intend to mortgage.

3 The maximum value of your loan will also depend on whether you are taking out a mortgage in your own name, or a joint-mortgage with a partner (or co-buyer). A typical multiple is two-and-a-half times the combined annual income.

4   To work out the maximum value of any property you can buy, take your mortgage ceiling and add the amount you have saved in cash to use as as a deposit (or the money you will have at your disposal following the sale of your current property).

5   Add to your monthly payments, the cost of mortgage insurance, any ground rent or service charge associated with the property, Council Tax for the area (you'll need to know the Council Tax band for that property) and an estimate of the utility costs, such as gas, electricity and water.

6   Compare this figure with your monthly net income to work out whether the mortgage is affordable.

✱ Tip

If you have regular monthly debt payments (for example, car loans or credit cards), take these into account when determining that bottom-line affordability figure.

⚠ Warnings

Lenders can only tell you what you might be able to afford based on your salary and debt level. You also have to feel comfortable with the reality of the monthly payment.

Don't assume that you can cut back your expenses and stretch yourself into a house payment. You can only live on beans on toast for so long.

If you take out a variable rate mortgage, be aware of the possible impact of a sudden increase in interests rate: When rates are around 5 per cent, a 25-year £200,000 repayment mortgage will require around £1,000 a month to be paid; if interest rates creep up to 7.5 per cent, your monthly payment will increase to around £1,500. Can your income sustain such an increase?

✓ 30 Evaluate a Neighbourhood

Property experts always say that the three most important things to consider when evaluating a property are location, location and location. That's because a home in a fashionable area with convenient shopping and good schools nearby will hold its value far better than an identical home in a less popular neighbourhood. Of course, it will also be much more pleasant to live in. Ask these questions to determine the quality of the neighbourhood you're considering, and to evaluate other local factors that go into making a house a good home – and a good investment.

- ☐ How well do residents keep up their properties?

- ☐ What is the ratio of renters to owners?

- ☐ How far away is the nearest shopping area? Is it easy to get to at the times you'll need to go?

- ☐ What is the quality of the local schools?

- ☐ Are local streets well-maintained?

- ☐ How much traffic is there? Is it safe for children?

- ☐ Is public transport nearby? Will it take you where you want to go?

- ☐ Is there a motorway or major road accessible from the area?

- ☐ How close are the nearest parks? Do they suit your family's needs?

- ☐ How close and accessible are cultural and entertainment facilities – theatres, museums and sports arenas?

- ❏ Visit the area after nightfall. Does it feel safe? How noisy is it?

- ❏ Check with the local police station. How much crime is there in the neighbourhood?

- ❏ Check with any local organisations. Is it a neighbourhood watch area?

- ❏ Check a map. How far is the nearest fire station or police station?

- ❏ Is there emergency medical service in the area?

- ❏ How far away is the nearest hospital? Is it close enough for your needs?

- ❏ Are you in the flight path of an airport? (Note that flight paths may change with weather conditions or at different times of day.)

- ❏ Is a fire station or train station so close as to cause noise pollution?

- ❏ If you are looking at a flat, check out any rules or regulations affecting the block. How do these fit in with your own style of decorating or living?

- ❏ Visit the council offices. Are any major new developments planned? What impact will these have on traffic, noise and school systems?

Make an Offer on a House

So you've found your dream home, looked it over carefully, and are now ready to make your offer. Here are the steps you'll need to take.

⊚ Steps

1. Consult a lender or mortgage broker to find out how much you can afford to spend on a house, or use a calculator on a financial website (see 29 "Determine How Big a Mortgage You Can Afford").

2. The amount you can borrow will vary from lender to lender, and will depend on whether you are taking out a mortgage on your own or a joint-mortgage with a partner (or co-buyer). A typical figure for the UK is three to four times one income, or two to three times a joint income.

3. Know how much money you have for a deposit. This will usually be at least 10 per cent (although in some cases first-time buyers may be able to secure a 100 per cent mortgage).

4. Decide what type of financing you want.

5. Know how much money you have for a down payment; typically 5 to 20 per cent of the purchase price is required, depending on the loan terms.

6. Make an offer to the vendor (or vendor's estate agent).

7. When approved, contact your solicitor to deal with contractual issues.

8. Now is the time to make a formal application for a mortgage.

△ Warning

Consult a solicitor before you sign anything. What you agree to could severely limit the remedies available to you by law.

32

Get Your House Ready to Sell

If your house makes a good impression on buyers, your chances of selling it faster and for more money are greater.

◎ Steps

1. Make any required repairs and keep a copy of the list (along with receipts) to share with buyers.

2. Choose little fixes that make a big difference. Replace old grouting in the kitchens and bathrooms; retouch paintwork, and repaint if necessary; get carpets cleaned; get rid of clutter; use brighter lightbulbs and open curtains to make rooms look bigger; get rid of pet smells.

3. Decide on which upgrades to make – such as replacing old, worn carpet; or replacing old sink, taps and light fixtures.

4. Make the entrance grand. First impressions are important.

5. Make sure your garden is in top shape.

⚠ Warning

Don't spend too much money on changes that won't enhance your bottom line.

33

Use an Estate Agent to Sell a House

Contrary to popular opinion, estate agents are not (necessarily) the spawn of Satan. Unless you relish the challenges of selling a house on your own, you'll need a professional to assist.

◎ Steps

1. Ask friends and families for a personal recommendation.

2   Make sure that any agent you consider belongs to a professional body, such as the National Association of Estate Agents. The NAEA sets certain standards for its members.

3   Look for estate agents who sell properties like yours – they will be more knowledgeable about that market and attract more suitable buyers. Look at the window displays of estate agents. Will your property get a clear photo with good details? Where do they advertise?

4   A good agent should know the local area well, and be able to show you examples of similar properties they've sold recently. Agents use comparisons to make their valuations, which can be difficult if your home is in some way unusual – all the more reason to use an agent who has recently sold a property like yours.

5   Interview at least three prospective estate agents before making a choice. Go with the agent you feel most confident with – not necessarily the one with the highest valuation.

6   You don't have to use just one agent. However, if you give sole selling rights to one agent, the commission you pay will be lower.

7   Expect to pay between 1.5 per cent and 2.5 per cent of the selling price, depending on the area. Some may agree to a flat fee, which may be a good deal on an expensive property.

⚠ Warnings

Beware of agents who suggest they can get an unreasonably high sales price. An agent might use a high valuation to get your business, and then seek a lower price later.

Be aware that VAT is payable on estate agent's fees.

34
Sell Your House Without an Agent

With a little savvy and a lot of tenacity, you can sell your house yourself – and save those commission costs.

◎ Steps

1   Set a fair price for your house. Study the sale prices of comparable

houses in your neighbourhood. (You can get this information from a local estate agent or newspaper.)

2 Use internet directory sites such as Fish4.co.uk and myhouseprice.com to find out how actual sale prices compare to asking prices – use this as a guide to your "bottom line".

3 Clean your house thoroughly and get rid of all clutter (see 32 "Get Your House Ready to Sell").

4 Advertise in local or specialised newspapers.

5 Use a solicitor to handle the contractual side of the deal.

⚠ Warning

Take the time to thoroughly understand contracts and discuss anything you don't fully understand with a solicitor.

35

Buy to Let

With mortgage rates enjoying a record low, why not consider buying a second property with the intention of renting it out. Buying to let gives you an asset that will (probably) increase in value as well as bringing in an additional monthly income.

◎ Steps

1 Consider your finances. Even if you already have a mortgage, some building societies will give you a second mortgage for such projects. Common among couples is for each partner to carry a separate mortgage.

2 Choose your property carefully. Areas with a high student population are usually a good bet.

3 As a landlord you have a legal responsibility to provide accommodation that comes up to environmental health standards. You may have to spend money on a property to get it up to scratch.

4 Decide if you really want the hassle of maintaining another property. If you live far away from your new property, or you are short of free

time, it may be worth paying a letting agent to deal with business on your behalf – but expect to pay up to 20 per cent of your potential rent in fees.

❋ Tip

If you have a son or daughter about to attend university, consider buying a house to let in that area. Not only will it provide "free" accommodation for your child – and allow them to choose and vet suitable house-mates – but you will also have someone living on hand to protect your investment and collect rent on your behalf.

36
Buy a Holiday Home

Buying a holiday home is exciting, but, as with any other major purchase, it's important to think things through carefully.

❋ Steps

1. Decide whether this is a place where you'd like to spend every holiday. If you're not sure, then it's probably not wise to buy.

2. Select the type of holiday home that best suits your needs.

3. Visit desired locations and tour properties for sale.

4. Determine whether the holiday property you are considering buying is priced fairly. Check local estate agents and newspapers to get a feel for the value of properties in the area. The process is then the same for buying any other property (see 28 "Buy a House").

5. Consider how you will maintain the holiday property throughout the year. Consider using a letting agent; a cheaper alternative is to find a reliable neighbour prepared to keep an eye on the place for you.

❋ Tips

You may get a better deal if you buy during the off-season.

If you're seeking a time-share, look on the internet for people selling their weeks independently.

37

Move Out of the City to the Country

Fed up with the pace of the big city? How about stepping back and taking in the country air?

◉ Steps

1. Leaving the rat-race behind is one of *the* great romantic dreams, but don't get carried away with the moment – make sure that you act with a clear head.

2. Consider the practicalities. What about your career? Can you commute to your existing job? Can you work from home? If not, do you have the financial resources to support yourself while you seek alternative employment.

3. Think about your lifestyle. Most cities have a wealth of amenities – music venues, restaurants, theatres, cinemas, health clubs – that are lacking in more isolated areas. If you enjoy a busy social life, the peace and quiet may be appealing, but will you miss it in the long term?

4. How practical are you? Be aware that you may have to deal with many everyday household problems on your own – there might not be a handy local plumber to fix a burst pipe for you, for instance.

⚠ Warning

Be aware that the desire to "get away" may be symptomatic of a deeper underlying problem – if you're running away from something the problem is likely to catch up with you eventually.

Personal Finance

Buy a Property Abroad

Once upon a time, buying a house abroad was only for the rich. But with house prices in much of mainland Europe substantially lower than in the UK, it has become possible for those of more modest means.

Steps

1. Overseas property seekers are often looking for sea and sun, so the coastline tends to be the most popular – and expensive.

2. Apply the same rules as if purchasing in the UK. Don't act on a whim. Do plenty of research. Start off by taking a holiday in the area you're considering. Are there enough facilities for what you require? Or do tourist attractions out-number the local amenities? The best source of knowledge is those who have done it before: there is no shortage of "ex-pats" with stories from which you can learn.

3. Unless you're fluent in the local language, conduct your enquiries through a reputable third party. In London and the South East there are many reputable estate agents who are expert in dealing with overseas properties. Use established companies and beware of anyone who gives you the hard sell.

4. Make sure you have a good lawyer with an excellent command of English and the local language to deal with the endless stream of rules and regulations. (In Spain, for instance, you can inherit debts from a previous vendor.)

5. Make sure you have the finances in place before you put in an offer. You may find it difficult to get a mortgage in the UK to pay for a foreign home. Take professional advice on the best way to arrange finances.

6. Start a direct debit from a local bank account to pay your regular utility bills. (Be aware that some foreign banks are considerably less lenient on late payers than the UK.)

7. Be aware that if you intend to remain resident in Britain, and wish to rent out your overseas property when it's empty, you could find yourself with income tax demands from both countries.

Seek out "ex-pat" clubs and societies to get first-hand experiences from those who have been there and done it before you.

⚠ Warning

If acting independently, you must make sure that you understand your obligations under local legislation. Wherever you happen to be in the world, when dealing with the law, ignorance is never a defence.

39

Decide Whether to Live Abroad

Many of us dream about leaving the country in search of a new way of life. In doesn't have to be very difficult to turn this dream into reality – as long as you are aware of the pitfalls.

◎ Steps

1 Decide where you want to live, and try to imagine your day-to-day life in a new country.

2 Many people contemplate such a move after returning from their holidays. Be aware that a great time spent as a tourist is usually a rather different experience than being permanent resident.

3 Find out if it's possible to make such a move. Does the country in which you want to live have entry regulations? Australia, for instance, has a points system based on personal factors such as education or career. Others may take your wealth into consideration.

4 Scour the internet in search of people who have already made the move. Learn from their experiences.

5 Consider practical issues. Can you speak the native tongue? Will you be able to work? Is there a demand for your profession? Will your children be able to resume school without major disruption?

6 Contact the embassy for the country in question. Many of those that are actively seeking to recruit will produce useful information packs. At the very least they will be able to advise you of any unique pitfalls.

Careers

Think carefully before committing yourself wholesale to a new way of life. Instead of selling up, why not rent out your home until you're satisfied that you want to make the permanent move?

40

Improve Your Memory

Scores of books, videos, web sites and seminars are devoted to memory enhancement. The steps below summarise the main points of most techniques.

Steps

1 Make sure you're alert and attentive before trying to memorise anything.

2 Understand the material rather than merely memorising it, if it's the type that requires deeper comprehension.

3 Look for larger patterns or ideas, and organise pieces of information into meaningful groups.

4 Link newly acquired knowledge with what you already know. Place what you learn into context with the rest of your knowledge, looking out for relationships between ideas.

5 Engage your visual and auditory senses by using drawings, charts or music to aid memory. Creating a memorable mental picture can also help.

6 Use mnemonics – devices such as formulas or rhymes that serve as memory aids. For example, use the acronym "HOMES" to memorise America's Great Lakes (Huron, Ontario, Michigan, Erie and Superior).

7 Repeat and review what you've learned as many times as you can. Apply it or use it in conversation, as continual practice is the key to remembering things in the long term.

Review the things you have memorised just before going to sleep; this might help you recall it better in the morning.

Things that interest you are easier to remember. Try to develop an interest in what you're memorising.

Your memory and thinking will function much better if you're in good health, well-rested and properly hydrated.

Try writing down or reciting aloud what you've memorised – this can help etch it in your mind.

41

Read Quickly and Effectively

Sail through the barrage of information out there by using some key reading and skimming skills.

⊙ **Steps**

1   Read different materials at different speeds: skim or speed-read less important items, and save critical or difficult works for when you are most alert and have time.

2   Pick out the main ideas of a book by reading the blurb on the jacket or scanning the table of contents. Use the index to locate key words quickly.

3   Survey the layout of your reading material. Look at the title and section headings and piece together its logical flow. This framework will guide you in reading the piece more carefully.

4   If you need to skim, try reading the first sentence of each paragraph (which is usually a topic sentence) to get a general idea of its content.

5   Practise reading more quickly by moving your index finger down a row of text at a speed slightly faster than your normal reading speed.

6   Underline sparingly so the truly useful information doesn't get lost.

7   Jot down quick notes, questions or thoughts that will make it easier to refer to the material later. Taking notes also makes for active reading and better retention of important points.

Increasing your vocabulary will help you to improve your reading speed.

Take a speed-reading course – there are many available.

42

Break the Procrastination Habit

There's an old joke that the members of Procrastinators Anonymous plan to meet ... but keep putting it off.

Steps

1. Think about why you procrastinate: Are you afraid of failing at the task? Are you a perfectionist and only willing to begin working after every little element is in place? Are you easily distracted?

2. Break up a large, difficult project into several smaller pieces.

3. Set deadlines for completion. Try assigning yourself small-scale deadlines: for example, commit to reading a certain number of pages in the next hour.

4. Work in small blocks of time instead of in long stretches. Try studying in one- to two-hour spurts, allowing yourself a small break after each stint.

5. Start with the easiest aspect of a large, complex project. For example, if you're writing an academic paper and find that the introduction is turning out to be difficult to write, start with the paper's body instead.

6. Enlist others to help. Make a bet with your family, friends or co-workers that you will finish a particular project by a specified time, or find other ways to make yourself accountable.

7. Eliminate distractions or move to a place where you can concentrate. Turn off the television, the phone bell, the radio and anything else that might keep you from your task.

Remember that progress, not perfection, is your goal.

43
Find Out Your IQ

Though IQ (intelligence quotient) has come under scrutiny as a measure of intelligence, finding out your IQ can help you join certain organisations and can open other doors for you.

⊙ Steps

1　Find an appropriate IQ test – there are a great many out there. On the web, consider visiting iqtest.com to take an IQ test and to get general information about the process.

2　Take the test and score it.

3　Take several more tests and average the scores, dropping the lowest and highest. The result will give a good approximation of your IQ.

4　Understand the results. Generally, an IQ of 100 places you in the 50th percentile (exactly average); 110 puts you in the 75th percentile; 120 in the 93rd; and 130 in the 98th, which is high enough to join Mensa.

5　Remember that no single number can measure something as complex as intelligence. Instead, IQ is intended to measure your chances of academic success in schools.

 Tip

Be aware that high-IQ societies such as Mensa usually accept the results of only certain IQ tests. Contact individual societies to find out its requirements (see 44 "Join Mensa").

⚠ Warning

Bear in mind that there are many important human "intelligences" that standard IQ tests can't measure, such as musical or artistic talent, social ability, physical coordination, ambition and sense of humour.

Join Mensa

Mensa is an international organisation of people in the top two per cent of the intelligence range. Founded in England in 1946, it now has more than 100,000 members. Here's how to join.

Steps

1. Bear in mind that having a test result in the top two per cent on an accepted IQ test or standardised test is the only membership criterion.

2. Visit the Mensa website (mensa.org.uk) to get the information you'll need to complete the steps below. Alternatively, call 01902 772771 or send a letter to British Mensa Limited, St John's House, St John's Square, Wolverhampton, WV2 4AH.

3. Find out if Mensa will accept the results of an intelligence test you've already taken. Mensa also accepts scores from approximately 200 standardised tests (such as the LSAT or GMAT).

4. Order official test results from the appropriate testing company and send them to Mensa.

5. Contact your nearest Mensa office to take the official Mensa test, if you haven't qualified through another test.

6. Be prepared to pay annual fees if you're admitted.

Tips

Visit Mensa's website to get more detailed information for your specific situation.

As a Mensa member, you'll be able to interact with other Mensa members at social events, through publications and during various activities.

Get a Job

Good timing plays a role in finding a job, but that's only part of the picture. Here's how to find the job you want.

Steps

1 Assess your skills, experience and goals, and look into appropriate employment fields that interest you.

2 Spread the word. Tell everyone you know and meet that you are looking for a job – you will be surprised at the number of opportunities you may discover this way.

3 Network, network, network. Attend professional-association meetings in your industry, scour the associations' membership directories for contacts, and schedule informational interviews with people in the field. Always try to get more names of people to contact at the end of the informational interview. Volunteer for something.

4 For resources and leads, contact your local employment office or your school/university careers advisor.

5 Get out and about. The most direct way to learn about job openings is to contact employers themselves. Target an area, dress the part, and stop in at every appropriate business establishment, including employment agencies, to fill out an application.

6 Remember that many job openings are not listed in the newspaper job section. However, internet job boards are often used by employers for their ease and immediacy.

7 Pick up the telephone. It may be scary – and you will hear "No" a lot – but you may only need to hear "Yes" a few times to land a job.

8 Follow up on written contacts. Send out CVs and fill out applications, but understand that these alone won't land you a job. Follow up with a phone call within five to seven days of every written communication.

9 Ask for interviews. If you find yourself being interviewed for a position that's not right for you (or with an interviewer who doesn't think you're right for the opening), request interviews with other department heads for resources and leads, or even with other companies that the interviewer may know are recruiting.

Careers

10 Prepare. Do some research on the hiring company and its industry so that you'll have a stock of relevant questions to ask the person across the desk.

11 Give the impression that you're ready to be part of the team.

12 Send a thank-you note after the interview. E-mail is acceptable.

13 Call your interviewer three days later and ask if there is any further information you can provide.

✻ Tips

When you're interviewing, make it a dialogue. Asking questions will make you appear knowledgeable and eager, as well as help to calm your nerves.

Review the Sunday job section to get a feel for the hiring marketplace.

Drop in on your local chamber of commerce breakfast or after-dinner meeting. These are usually open to non-members for a small fee and offer the opportunity to make valuable contacts.

See 49 "Speed Up a Job Hunt" for additional pointers.

⚠ Warning

Avoid making the mistake of turning down additional interviews once you've had a good one. Keep your job search in high gear right up until your first day on the new job.

46

Find a Job Online

The internet is rewriting the rules of the job-search game. Make sure that you know all the ways to find a job online.

⊚ Steps

1 Peruse the websites of any companies that may interest you. Most companies will post job openings on their sites.

2 Go to a website specifically geared towards finding jobs. You can search for jobs on these sites by career field, location and even potential salary.

3   If you're a student, your school or university may have a careers advice web page with job listings, guidance for writing CVs and advice on being interviewed.

4   Visit an online newspaper and search the classifieds section for job adverts and job opportunities. Many newspapers – national and local – have web pages.

5   Check out search engines, as these also feature classified sections. Browse according to your location and interests.

 Tips

Search frequently: new job listings are posted every day.

Many sites offer services that will allow you to e-mail your cv directly to a potential employer.

⚠ **Warning**

Some sites designed specifically for finding jobs may require a membership fee. Read the small print before signing up.

47
Network Effectively

Networking can help you to get a job or otherwise expand your business horizons. The key to successful networking is taking the initiative – and refining your conversational skills.

◉ **Steps**

1   Talk to people you don't know, everywhere you go. Cocktail parties and weddings are just the tip of the iceberg; don't forget about aeroplanes, supermarket queues, sports events, festivals, bookshops and so on.

2   Learn to ask "What do you do?" with comfort, sincerity and interest.

3   Become a better listener. Ask a question and then be quiet until you hear the answer.

4   Practise the way you present your own skills. Learn more than one approach, whether frank or subtle.

5 Keep a great updated brochure, business card or some other form of information about yourself on you at all times. Get comfortable with handing out your card.

6 Take classes to improve your public speaking, body language and writing skills.

7 Join every networking club and association in your field.

8 Follow up on any lead, no matter how minor.

✱ Tips

Make news so that you can get your name out there. Be the dog walker who gets on the evening news for organising the Doggy Olympics.

Stay in touch with people you like and respect even if they can't help you immediately. You don't want to go to someone only when you are desperate.

48

Prepare a Basic CV

There are as many kinds of CV as there are jobs. Use a style that matches your personality and career objectives.

◉ Steps

1 Choose one or two fonts at most, and avoid underlined, boldfaced and italic text. Some companies use automated recruiting systems that have difficulty with special formatting.

2 Opt for the active voice rather than the passive voice (say "met the goal" rather than "the goal was met").

3 Provide contact information such as your home address, telephone number and e-mail address at the top of your CV.

4 Include an objectives statement, in which you use clear, simple language to indicate what kind of job you're looking for. This should appear below your contact information.

5 List your most recent and relevant experience first. Include time frames, company names and job titles, followed by major responsibilities.

6   In a second section, outline your education, awards, accomplishments and anything else you wish prospective employers to know about you.

7   Hire a proofreader or ask someone you trust to proofread your CV. Mistakes in spelling, grammar or syntax can land it in the bin.

8   Limit your CV to one page unless it is scientific or highly technical. Less is definitely more when it comes to CVs.

9   Write a covering letter to submit with your CV

 Tips

Refrain from using "I" in your CV.

Leave out personal information, particularly relating to your age, race, religious background and sexual orientation.

Avoid obscure fonts, clip art and other unnecessary visuals.

✓ 49 Speed Up a Job Hunt

When you're looking for a job, it's all too easy to let yourself be lulled by the familiar rhythms of home or work life. Before you know it, another month has gone by and you're still out of work or unhappily employed. Here are some ways to jump-start your job search and get your career in gear.

Know yourself

- ☐ Make a list of your skills. Note which ones you're most interested in using, and which are most likely to interest employers.

- ☐ Identify the skills that you haven't had the chance to use in your current or most recent job. Which ones are of greatest importance to you?

- ☐ Think about how you can use your favourite skills in a new job. Set specific short-term and long-term goals to guide your job search.

- ☐ Decide which of your short-term goals are negotiable and which are not.

- ☐ Write a two-minute speech describing your experience, skills and goals. Rehearse it.

Brush up job-seeking skills

- ☐ Hire a proofreader to catch any errors in your CV.

- ☐ Ask a friend or colleague to grill you about your experience so you can practise your answers.

- ☐ Videotape yourself in a mock interview to see how you come across.

- ☐ Hire a consultant to look at your CV and teach you some interview techniques.

- ☐ Make sure you have clean, wrinkle-free professional attire ready to wear for job interviews.

Get organised

- ☐ Make a list of leads: people you know, people they've referred you to and companies that interest you.

- ☐ Set goals – for example, to send out ten CVs this week, make five cold calls or conduct two informational interviews.

- ☐ Make weekly and daily to-do lists, and check off each item as it's completed.

- ☐ Keep files or notebooks with details of everyone you've written to, called or who has interviewed you, and anything you want to remember. Include job listings and contacts' business cards.

- ☐ Keep your filing system handy and well-organised so you can refer to it quickly in case of a phone call.

Research and target employers

- ☐ Read trade publications to learn about companies in your field and determine which ones may be hiring.

- ☐ Talk to friends or acquaintances in the field for the inside scoop on companies.

- ☐ Set up informational interviews or ask to spend a day with someone who has the type of job you're seeking.

- ☐ Aim your cover letters to individuals who may be in a position to hire you – send a copy to the personnel department as well.

- ☐ After scheduling an interview, search the web for more facts about the company.

- ☐ Ask the company for a press kit or annual report if it's not available on the web.

- ☐ Make a list of questions that show your knowledge and interest in the company.

Succeed at a Job Interview

Most interviewers form their opinion of you in the first few minutes of a meeting. Here's how to make a good impression.

Steps

1. In the days before your interview, talk to people who have worked at the company. If it's practical, hang around outside the building while employees are arriving and note how they dress and behave.

2. Learn the name and title of the person you'll be meeting. Arrive at least ten minutes early to collect your thoughts.

3. Take time to greet and acknowledge the secretary or administrative assistant; it's good old-fashioned courtesy, and besides, this person may have a lot of influence.

4. Bring along an extra copy of your CV or letters of recommendation in case the interviewer doesn't have them handy.

5. Be open and upbeat. Face your interviewer with arms and legs uncrossed, head up, and hands and face at ease. Smile and look the interviewer in the eye.

6. Know the company's business, target clients, market and direction.

7. Walk in prepared with a few relevant questions and listen carefully.

8. Subtly give the impression that you're already part of the team by using "we" when asking how something is done. For example, say, "How do we deal with the press?"

9. Conclude with a positive statement and a quick, firm handshake. Ask when you might follow up, and get a business card from the interviewer.

10. Send a thank-you note.

Tip

Avoid asking about money at the start of the interview.

Request a Reference From a Former Employer

A good employment reference can seal that job offer that you've worked hard to win.

Steps

1. Get references before you need them. Managers make job changes, too, and time can erase the memory of even the most outstanding employee.

2. Offer to write the reference letter for your former employer to review and sign. This saves him or her valuable time, and it allows you to highlight the accomplishments you consider most valuable to future employers.

3. Contact former employers and other referees before offering their names to potential employers. Beyond simple courtesy, this gives you the chance to supply these people with important information such as who might be calling, the type of job you're applying for, and which of your skills you would like your referee to emphasise.

4. Acknowledge a referee with a thank-you note, even if you didn't get the job. If you did, offer a celebratory lunch.

Tips

If you encounter an unhelpful policy, such as one that restricts managers from giving reference information beyond confirming job title and relevant dates of employment, ask the manager if he or she will give you a personal (rather than professional) reference.

Consider colleagues with whom you've interacted – they can be good referees, too.

Negotiate an Employment Contract

Be confident and careful when negotiating a new contract.

Steps

1. Research your market value before your first interview: Talk to friends and acquaintances in the business, contact headhunters, and consult career web pages that include information such as salary ranges and benefits packages.

2. Assess the company's approach, noting whether it invites negotiations or makes an offer first.

3. Listen to the way an offer is presented. A negotiation-minded manager will ask what figure you had in mind to get the process moving.

4. Delineate the different aspects of the job offer: money, benefits, share options, responsibilities, schedules.

5. If the offer appears set, be creative in negotiating for alternative perks such as time off, relocation expenses or a travel allowance.

6. Repeat the offer out loud after you hear it, then don't say anything until the employer does. Your silence may be misinterpreted as hesitation and the employer will sweeten the pot.

7. Speak your mind if you have any concerns.

Tips

Clearly demonstrate your sincere excitement and interest in the job as well as in the compensation.

Focus on being an ally – not an adversary – throughout the negotiations. This will keep things amiable and show that you are a team player.

Work Efficiently

We'll keep this short so you can get back to work.

◎ Steps

1 Keep your desk and your files organised to avoid wasting time shuffling through piles of paper.

2 Go through your inbox at the beginning of each workday. Either throw away, file or follow up on each item.

3 Prioritise a list of the tasks you need to accomplish that day.

4 Delegate tasks to co-workers and assistants if possible.

5 Finish one task before you go on to the next.

6 Reduce paperwork by storing important information on your computer or electronic organiser.

7 Communicate effectively and plan carefully to make sure a job is done properly the first time around.

8 Schedule time when you'll be available and let colleagues know, to avoid constant interruptions. Close the door if you need to.

9 Take breaks. A short walk or quick lunch away from the office will increase your overall productivity.

10 Before leaving for the day, tidy up your desk and make a short list of projects you will need to do the next day.

11 Try not to take work home. You need the break.

✳ Tips

Recognise when you have the most energy in a day and do the important or harder tasks then.

Note that certain days – usually Monday or Friday – are more hectic, and schedule accordingly.

Have someone else answer your telephone if possible. Give instructions about calls you wish to take and those that can be returned later.

Careers

Avoid regularly going out for long business lunches – heavy meals make for unproductive afternoons.

Avoid procrastination (see 42 "Break the Procrastination Habit").

54

Make a To-Do List

Invest just a little time planning your day, and accomplish more things smoothly.

◉ Steps

1. Set aside 10 to 15 minutes before you go to bed or as soon as you wake up in the morning to jot down a to-do list for the day.

2. Use any format that is comfortable for you – try writing in your daily planner. Make sure your list is on one page and can be carried with you wherever you go.

3. Try assigning tasks to hourly time slots, even if exact timing isn't crucial.

4. Fill in preset, mandatory appointments such as business meetings or child-pickup times.

5. Prioritise tasks in order of urgency, and write those down before less important ones.

6. Figure out when, during the day, you are most productive and alert. Schedule the more demanding tasks during these times.

7. Schedule an easy job after a difficult one or a long task after a short one to keep yourself stimulated.

8. Indicate time for breaks and time to spend with family and friends.

9. In addition to your daily schedule, keep an ongoing list of projects that you need to accomplish but haven't pencilled into your daily list – things to fix around the house, bills to post, people to call. Update this list at least once a week.

10 Keep a list of long-term goals. For example, you might be planning to renovate your home or return to university for an advanced degree.

11 Make a running list for leisure or entertainment goals – books to read, films to rent, restaurants/bars/clubs to try. Write down names as you hear or read about them.

✳ Tips

Schedule things comfortably, allowing time for unexpected delays or mishaps; avoid an impossibly tight timetable.

Be sure to list everything you need to accomplish – the more you can account for, the more smoothly your day will run and the less you need to remember.

Break down large projects into specific tasks before writing them down on your list.

Feel free to revise your list as necessary, as the day goes on.

55

Get Promoted

Promotion is about more than just doing a good job and hoping that your boss notices your huge potential.

◉ Steps

1 Your biggest clue is in the word "promote". In the workplace, make sure that your strengths and potential are well advertised to colleagues and senior staff.

2 Feel confident that you know every aspect of your current position.

3 Be aware of vacant jobs within your organisation – at the very least, this will show your interest and commitment to the company. Find out as much as you can about any position that interests you.

4 Be seen as smart, punctual and reliable, and willing to take on extra tasks if necessary.

5 Be prepared to work beyond your normal hours if necessary – why would anyone want to promote a "clockwatcher"?

Careers

6   Carry out your day-to-day tasks with enthusiasm. It's much easier to get on if you're liked by those around you.

7   Use meetings, conferences and appraisals as opportunities to shine.

 Tip

Take any training opportunities you are offered – it shows that you want to get on. Seek others out for yourself.

⚠ Warning

There's a delicate line between "selling" yourself and outright bragging. Tread that line with care – you don't want to come across as an arrogant git!

56

Ask for a Pay Rise

Consider whether you merit a pay rise and whether your company is in a position to give you one. Then choose your moment and your methods carefully.

◎ Steps

1   Evaluate your worth. List your achievements, skills and contributions.

2   Arm yourself with information. Know what a normal rise is for someone of your experience and occupation.

3   Assess your superior's mood and outlook. Do you think he or she is ready to consider your request?

4   Choose an appropriate time of day. Make an appointment or ask if there are a few minutes to spare. Plan for an end-of-business-day meeting.

5   Consider asking for a specific amount that's a little higher than you want. Say "eight per cent" when you would be happy with six.

6   Be realistic. If your company is going through tough times but you still feel deserving, decide how you'll respond if a lower amount is offered.

7   Be flexible. Would you consider a supplement in perks, time off, flexible time or holiday time in lieu of a rise? Negotiate.

8   If your superior turns you down, have a back-up plan ready.

 Tip

If you can, print out an outline showing that you're paid less than others in your position – but are producing more and better results.

⚠ Warning

Avoid losing your temper or your sense of humour.

57

Get on TV

You thought that being on TV was just for superstars? Maybe it's about time you stepped out in front of the cameras – even if it is standing behind a court reporter outside the Old Bailey.

◎ Steps

1   Are you really good at anything? So good that it would simply be a crime if you failed to share your talents with the world? That's still probably (just about) the best way to get on TV. If not, perhaps it's *Big Brother* for you.

2   Do you have any major problems? If so, researchers on such talk shows as *Now You're Talking* (bbc.co.uk) or *Trisha* (angliatv.com/trisha) are just waiting to hear from you. And remember: the weirder – and more sordid – the better your chances of appearing.

3   Ever wondered who all those "nobodies" are that routinely wander in the background scenes of your favourite shows? If you fancy being spotted wandering through Albert Square or down Coronation Street then you'll need to register with an "extras" agency – do a search on the internet, or try tv-filmextras.co.uk or extras.tv/information.htm.

4   Are you unusual to look at, or even – to be blunt – downright ugly? There are a number of modelling agencies that specialise in finding "character" faces for TV shows or commercials – try Ugly (ugly.org).

Fun Activities

Being on TV, especially as the star of a reality show, may sound like a good idea at the time, but it can seriously backfire.

Remember, the "stars" of these programmes are often only noted for one thing and it's generally not for being Brain of Britain.

58

Be in the Audience for a TV Show

A night out at the theatre or comedy club can cost an arm and a leg these days, especially if it's a big name you want to see. But how would you fancy a night out that doesn't cost you a penny? Interested?

Steps

1. Look at the BBC's ticketing web pages (bbc.co.uk/whatson/tickets). Here you can find a list of all the TV and radio shows that are being recorded over the coming months. You can make your choices and order the tickets online. For shows broadcast on Channel 4, you can order tickets from channel4.com/tickets.html.

2. Some shows are produced independently. At the end of a programme's credits, make a note of the production company. You should be able to find a contact either by doing a web search or looking it up in one of the many broadcasting industry directories – you'll find them in most public libraries.

※ Tip

As the shows are free it's not uncommon for people to order their tickets and not turn up. Consequently, many more tickets are usually sent out than can be accommodated in the theatre. Make sure that you arrive early since seating will be on a first come first served basis.

59

Be a Contestant on a Game Show

It doesn't matter whether it's *Who Wants To Be A Millionaire?* or *Family Fortunes*, for a TV game show to work it must have one vital ingredient – a contestant. It has to be someone, so why not you?

⊚ Steps

1. Identify the quiz show in which you want to take part. Have a pen and paper ready – often you will hear details of how to apply at the end of the show. If it's produced by an independent TV company, note the name – you may need to contact them later.

2. If the quiz show was broadcast on the BBC you should be able find details on the BBC web pages (bbc.co.uk); similarly with programmes made on Channel 4 (channel4.com), ITV (itv.com) and Channel 5 (channel5.co.uk).

3. Contact independent producers directly.

⚠ Warning

Be prepared for disappointment: contestants are not always chosen for their capabilities but for other characteristics, such as photogenic appearance or particular type of personality.

60

Spot Celebrities

Although it may sometimes seem as though they inhabit another world altogether, getting a good "star spot" may be easier than you think – you just need to look in the right places.

⊚ Steps

1. Think about where the stars are based. You'll clearly have a better chance of spotting a TV celebrity wandering around London's Soho than in a shopping centre in Swindon.

Fun Activities

2   Find out about film premieres and award ceremonies. That's where you'll find your favourite celebs looking their most glamourous.

3   Subscribe to the biggest celebrity magazines, such as *OK!* and *Heat*. Gossip columns will often talk about bars, hotels and restaurants where the rich and famous hang out. (If you can get a table at The Ivy in London, you're guaranteed a star spot: if you can't get a table – or can't afford one – hang around outside for a few hours.)

4   In recent years, it's become fashionable for some of Hollywood's biggest names to tread the boards on London's West End. So, if you know the theatre and are prepared to hang around by the stage door, you might just get a glimpse of such A-list stars as Kevin Spacey or Nicole Kidman.

5   Shop with the stars! Take a trip to some of London's coolest fashion houses. Every celeb's favourite department store? Forget Harrods – that's for the tourists – instead, head for Harvey Nichols. Indeed, any of the big designer names in Sloane Street have the potential to come up with the goods.

⚠ Warnings

There can be a fine line between spotting celebrities and turning into a stalker.

Not all stars like to be accosted by strangers, and so may not be as friendly as they seem on your favourite shows. Be aware that the experience could be a very disappointing one for you – for every Dustin Hoffman who'll happily talk to your Mum on your mobile phone, there'll be a Jay Kay ready to bloody your nose.

61
Whistle

If singing is not your biggest strength, try whistling your favourite tunes. Follow these steps and practise until you can whistle with comfort and ease.

◉ Steps

1   Purse your lips into a tiny O shape, leaving a small opening for air.

2   Place the tip of your tongue behind your bottom teeth or against your inside bottom gums.

3   Gently expel air through your mouth.

4   Adjust your tongue position and the small opening formed by your lips until you hear a note.

5   Once you can sound one note, experiment with your tongue position and the strength of your breath to produce different notes.

6   Practise!

❄ Tips

Try not to blow too hard at first; it's much easier to whistle with a small amount of air.

You may find it easier to produce a strong, pure note if you wet your lips first.

62

Waltz

The waltz, which evolved from a German folk dance, is danced to a triple beat. It is popular throughout Europe and the United States, especially at formal social events.

◎ Steps

1   Get into position by facing your partner. If you are the leader, place your right hand on your partner's waist slightly around the back and extend your left hand to your side with your elbow bent and your palm raised, facing her. With that hand, grasp your partner's right hand in a loose grip, and make sure your partner has her left hand on your right shoulder, with her elbow bent. She should mirror your movements.

2   On the first beat, step forwards gracefully with your left foot. Your partner should follow your lead by doing the opposite of what you do on each beat – in this case, stepping back with her right foot.

3   On the second beat, step forwards and to the right with your right foot. Trace an upside-down letter L in the air with your foot as you do this.

4   Shift your weight to your right foot. Keep your left foot stationary.

Fun Activities

5. On the third beat, slide your left foot over to your right and stand with your feet together.

6. On the fourth beat, step back with your right foot.

7. On the fifth beat, step back and to the left with your left foot, this time tracing a backward L. Shift your weight to your left foot.

8. On the final beat, slide your right foot towards your left until your feet are together. Now you're ready to start again with your left foot.

9. Repeat steps 2 to 8, turning your and your partner's orientation slowly to the left by slightly varying the placement of your feet.

✳ Tips

It helps to count as you go – "one, two, three; one, two, three" – placing the emphasis on the "one" as you count.

Practise to a slow waltz until you become comfortable with the moves.

63

Tango

Born in the brothels of Argentina, the tango is synonymous with passion. Although the dance is relatively free-form, you can do a lot with two basic moves: the walking step and the rock step.

◉ Steps

1. Face your partner and stand closer together than you would in most other ballroom dances – close enough for your torsos to touch.

2. If you're the leader, place your right hand on the middle of your partner's lower back. Extend your left hand out to your side with your arm bent and grasp your partner's right hand in a loose grip. Your partner should place her left hand on your right shoulder and place her right hand lightly in your palm with her right elbow bent.

3. On the first beat, walk forwards slowly with your left foot, placing down your heel first and then your toes. Your partner will mirror each of your movements on every beat throughout the dance – in this case, moving her right foot backwards, landing her toes and then her heel.

4   On the second beat, step forwards slowly with your right foot so that it moves past your left. You should feel as if you are slinking forwards.

5   On the third beat, step forwards quickly with your left foot, then immediately slide your right foot quickly to the right side and shift your weight to that foot.

6   On the fourth beat, bring your left foot slowly to your right, leaving your left leg slightly bent as your feet come together. Your weight should still be on your right foot.

7   Now, shift your weight to your left foot and do a right forwards rock step: While making a half-turn clockwise, step forwards quickly on your right foot, and then quickly shift your weight back to your left foot. With your right foot, slowly step forwards to complete the half turn.

8   Bring your feet together, bring your left foot up next to your right and repeat steps 3 to 7.

 Tips

Bear in mind that your feet barely leave the floor as you dance.

This isn't a subtle way to meet people.

64

Salsa

Listen to the rhythm of the music as you learn this popular Latin dance. You can learn the basic salsa steps in less than an hour, and sashay all over the dance floor before you know it.

⊙ Steps

1   Get in position by facing your partner. If you are the leader, place your right hand on your partner's waist, slightly around the back. Extend your left arm diagonally to chest height with your elbow bent at a right angle and your palm raised. Grasp your partner's right hand in a loose grip; your partner's left hand should be on your right shoulder.

2   On the first beat, step forwards with your left foot. Your partner will

Fun Activities

mirror each of your movements throughout the dance; for example, on the first beat she will step backwards with her right foot.

3   Step in place with your right foot on the second beat.

4   Step back with your left foot on the third beat so that you are back in the starting position, and hold in place for the fourth beat.

5   Step back with your right foot on the fifth beat.

6   Step in place with your left foot on the sixth beat.

7   Step forwards with your right foot on the seventh beat so that you are back in the starting position, and hold for the eighth beat.

8   Repeat, starting at step 2.

 Tips

You can add more complicated moves once you've grasped the basic salsa step.

Don't use exaggerated hip movement. That sexy swing will come naturally as you let yourself feel the rhythm.

Some salsa clubs offer free or inexpensive introductory classes or specials on certain nights of the week.

65

Jive

Modern jive is a dance style that evolved in the 1990s. It can be danced to many kinds of music, from rock'n'roll and swing to much of contemporary pop. There are hundreds of possible variations, but here is a basic move to get started.

Steps

1   Get in position by facing your partner. If you are the leader (usually the man), turn your hands palm upwards in front of you at waist level. Your partner lays her hands lightly over yours.

2   Initiate the dance with a step backwards by both partners. Bend your fingers to create a grip and stretch your arms so that you can feel the tension of your two bodies pulling away from one another. Keep the handhold light – neither of you should grip with your thumbs.

3   Step together on the next beat, at the same time turning anti-
    clockwise through 90 degrees, so that you are side by side.

4   Both twist 180 degrees clockwise on the next beat so that you are
    again side by side but facing in the opposite direction.

5   Both twist 90 degrees anti-clockwise to face one another. If you are
    the leader, raise your left hand to shoulder height. The partner mirrors
    this by raising her right hand. Ensure the hands are palm to palm,
    touching but not holding.

6   If you are the leader, push downwards to propel the partner into a
    spin. The partner spins through 360 degrees and returns to face the
    leader.

7   Resume the light grip with both hands and both step back, once more
    creating tension in the arms as you pull apart. You are ready to repeat
    the move or try another variant.

✳ Tips

Keep your arms at waist level most of the time. When pulling apart, don't
extend your arms out fully straight – if you do, the effect is jerky and
definitely uncool.

Some jive clubs offer inexpensive introductory classes on certain nights
of the week. You will need lessons to pick up enough moves to make
jiving worthwhile.

66

Write a Sonnet

The sonnet, a 14-line poem, has two main types: English (or
Shakespearean) and Italian (or Petrarchan). Here, we present
the format for writing a Shakespearean sonnet.

◉ Steps

1   Select the subject matter for your sonnet. Themes have often focused
    on love or philosophy, but modern sonnets can cover almost any
    topic.

2   Divide the theme of your sonnet into two sections. In the first section
    you will present the situation or thought to the reader; in the second
    section you can present some sort of conclusion or climax.

Fun Activities

3   Compose your first section as three quatrains – that is, three stanzas of four lines each. Write the three quatrains with an *a-b-a-b, c-d-c-d, e-f-e-f* rhyme scheme, where each letter stands for a line of the sonnet and the last words of all lines with the same letter rhyme with each other. Most sonnets employ the metre of iambic pentameter (see Tips), as seen in these three quatrains from Shakespeare's "Sonnet 30":

When to the sessions of sweet silent thought (a)
I summon up remembrance of things past, (b)
I sigh the lack of many a thing I sought, (a)
And with old woes new wail my dear time's waste: (b)
Then can I drown an eye, unus'd to flow, (c)
For precious friends hid in death's dateless night, (d)
And weep afresh love's long since cancell'd woe, (c)
And moan th'expense of many a vanish'd sight: (d)
Then can I grieve at grievances foregone, (e)
And heavily from woe to woe tell o'er (f)
The sad account of fore-bemoanéd moan, (e)
Which I new pay as if not paid before. (f)

4   Compose the last section as a couplet—two rhyming lines of poetry. This time, use a *g-g* rhyme scheme, where the last words of the two lines rhyme with each other. We refer once more to "Sonnet 30":

But if the while I think on thee, dear friend, (g)
All losses are restored and sorrows end. (g)

 Tips

An iamb is a type of metrical "foot" used in a poem. It is composed of two syllables, with the accent on the second syllable. Examples: "to*day*" or "en*rage*". Pentameter means that there are five metrical feet per line. Iambic pentameter means that each line of the poem consists of five iambic feet, or 10 total syllables. An example from Shakespeare: "Good pilgrim you do wrong your hand too much."

In the Italian sonnet, use an *a-b-b-a-a-b-b-a* rhyme scheme for the first section (called the "octave"), and a rhyme scheme of *c-d-e-c-d-e* or *c-d-c-d-c-d* in the second section (called the "sestet").

Write a Short Story

The model described here is the pyramid plot. The upward slope establishes setting and characters and builds tension; the tip is the climax; and the downward slope is the resolution.

◎ Steps

1. Choose a narrative point of view. You can write your story as if you were one of the characters (first person), as a detached narrator who presents just one character's thoughts and observations (third-person limited), or as a detached narrator who presents the thoughts and observations of several characters (third-person omniscient). A first-person point of view will refer to the central character as "I" instead of "he" or "she".

2. Create a protagonist, or main character. This should be the most developed and usually the most sympathetic character in your story.

3. Create a problem, or conflict, for your protagonist. The conflict of your story should take one of five basic forms: person vs. person, person vs. himself or herself, person vs. nature, person vs. society, or person vs. God or fate. If you choose a person vs. person conflict, create an antagonist to serve as the person your protagonist must contend with.

4. Establish believable characters and settings, with vivid descriptions and dialogue, to create a story that your readers will care about.

5. Build the story's tension by having the protagonist make several failed attempts to solve or overcome the problem. (You may want to miss out this step for shorter stories.)

6. Create a crisis that serves as the last chance for the protagonist to solve his or her problem.

7. Resolve the tension by having the protagonist succeed through his or her own intelligence, creativity, courage or other positive attributes. This is usually referred to as the story's climax.

8. Extend this resolution phase, if you like, by reflecting on the action of the story and its significance to the characters or society.

Fun Activities

There are many possible variations of this model, all of which allow for perfectly good short stories.

Keep your language concise, specific and active. For example, write "Steve ate the apple" instead of "The fruit was eaten by someone".

68

Write a Limerick

There once was a fellow called Larry,
Who sought to write lim'ricks for Carrie.
  With the help of eHow
  He wrote one, and now
Young Larry is married to Carrie.

Steps

1. Prepare to write five lines of verse. If you're stumped, try starting off your limerick with the traditional "There once was a ...".

2. Create the following stress pattern in lines one, two and five: da-*da* da-da-*da* da-da-*da*-da. For example, "There *once* was a *fel*-low called *Lar*-ry....". You can omit the last, unstressed syllable if you prefer.

3. Create the following stress pattern in lines three and four: da-*da* da-da-*da*. For example, "He *wrote* one, and *now*". You have the option of adding an extra unstressed syllable before the first stress and one or two syllables after the last stress.

4. Make sure your limerick's rhyme scheme is *a-a-b-b-a*. In other words, the first, second and fifth lines all rhyme with one another; the third and fourth lines rhyme with each other.

5. Exploit puns and wordplay.

Tips

The racier, the better. Limericks are notoriously bawdy and obnoxious.

The last line should deliver a punch, whether surprising, funny or naughty.

You can be flexible about rhythm as long as you make sure there are three strong beats in lines 1, 2 and 5, and two in lines 3 and 4.

Start a Collection

An informed collector is a happy collector. Know what you're buying and the best price before you buy the item.

◎ Steps

1. Work out what kind of items you are interested in collecting, or determine if you already have three or more of a certain object. You may have begun a collection without knowing it.

2. Subscribe to collecting magazines or newsletters that are devoted to your object(s) of interest.

3. Purchase books and do the research required to become an expert in your subject of interest. It will save you money in the long run because you'll recognise bargains and rip-offs when you see them.

4. Allocate a space in which to store the collection. It's best if this space is easily viewed so that you can enjoy the fruits of your obsession. Purchase display cases or shelves if necessary.

5. Set a budget so you don't spend too much money on the collection.

6. Use the internet or newsletters to form a loose network with other collectors and sellers.

7. Thoroughly research each item before you purchase it.

8. Keep a record of your contacts, the items in your collection and the date and cost of purchase.

✳ Tips

Monitor online auction sites, such as eBay, to find out general price ranges and typical rates.

Let family and friends know that you are starting a collection. It will help them come up with gift ideas for you.

Many collections can be assembled or started without making special purchases with items such as matchboxes, bottle caps, seashells or pine cones.

Fun Activities

Play Charades

Charades, believed to have originated in 18th-century France, is a classic party game that's fun for all ages. You'll need at least six people to play.

Steps

The Game

1. Divide the group into two teams of at least three people each. Decide on a time limit – between 3 and 5 minutes – for each round.

2. Ask each team to write titles of books, TV shows or movies, or other phrases (see Tips), on individual scraps of paper, then fold them to hide the writing. Each team then places its scraps in a separate bowl.

3. When it's your turn, close your eyes and pick a piece of paper from the other team's bowl. Read its contents to yourself.

4. Without speaking, help your team try to guess the title by giving signals using appropriate gestures (see the following section).

5. Stop when your team guesses the title or time runs out.

6. Sit down and watch the other team draw a title and act it out.

7. When it's your team's turn again, watch as one of your teammates draws a new title out of the bowl; now it's your turn to try to guess what your team mate is acting out.

8. Record how many clues it takes each team to guess correct titles (or add up the number of correct guesses per team) to determine the winner.

The Clues

1. To indicate a book title, put your hands together as if you are praying, then unfold them flat.

2. To indicate a film title, form an O with one hand to pantomime a lens while cranking the other hand as if you are operating an old-fashioned movie camera.

3. Indicate a television show by making a box with your fingers.

4   Make quotation marks in the air with your fingers to indicate a quote.

5   Pose like Napoleon (with a hand on your chest and the tips of your fingers tucked partway into your shirt) to indicate a famous person.

6   Pull on your ear to indicate that the word being guessed sounds like another word.

7   Hold up fingers to indicate the number of words in the title, quotation or name; hold up a number of fingers again to indicate which word you want your teammates to guess.

8   Hold fingers against your arm to indicate the number of syllables in a particular word.

9   Pinch your thumb and forefinger or open them up to indicate a short or long word.

10 Confirm that your partners have guessed a word correctly by tapping your index finger on your nose and pointing to the person or persons who made the correct guess.

11 Wipe your hand across your forehead to let your team mates know that they are getting warm.

12 Cross your arms and shiver to let them know that they are getting cold.

✳ Tips

In addition to book, film and TV titles, popular charades topics include well-known quotations, song titles and names of famous people, rock bands and places.

Arrange other signals with your partners before the game, if you wish, but remember that it's against the rules to arrange an "alphabet code" to act out the spelling of a word.

It is improper to point to people or objects in the room for hints.

71

Do a Cryptic Crossword Puzzle

Cryptic crosswords, such as the one that appears daily in **The Times**, are a source of lifelong pleasure for some people, but a complete mystery to others. Here are some clues to get started.

Fun Activities

1. Know that each clue normally consists of two parts, one that gives you a devious, riddling way to work out the solution, and the other that gives the literal meaning of the solution. For example, "Endless hate for headgear" would have the solution "hat". (Cryptically, the word "hate" without its end, or final letter, and also literally, "headgear".)

2. Try to work out which part of the clue gives the literal meaning, but remember that the most obvious answer is unlikely to be the right one!

3. Look out for anagrams – letters to unscramble – as these are often among the easier types of clue to solve. Anagrams are usually indicated by words such as "confused" or "changing" (clue: "Changing places? It is requiring particular skill"; solution: "specialist" – an anagram of "places it is", meaning "someone with a particular skill").

4. Look out for "hidden word" clues, where the solution is to be found in consecutive letters embedded in the clue. For example, clue: "Holdall found in cab again"; solution: "bag" (a holdall is a bag, and the word "bag" is found in "caB AGain".

5. Learn key words that are regularly used in clues with a special purpose. For example, "sailor" is often used to indicate the syllables "tar" or "ab" (nickname for a sailor and initials for "able-bodied seaman"); "flower" is very likely to mean "river" (get it?); "saint" or "holy man" may indicate the letters "st"; and so on.

6. Look at each clue as many ways as you can. Mental flexibility is the key to solving cryptic crosswords.

7. If you're stumped, put the puzzle down for a while and try again later.

8. Go through the correct solutions in the following day's newspaper. Compare the solutions with the clues and see if you can understand how the clues worked.

✱ Tips

Filling inspired guesses into the crossword square is often a useful way forwards for beginners. Use a pencil so that you can rub out mistakes easily.

A question mark at the end of a clue means that it is somehow especially devious. Such clues may not have the classic two-part structure of a cryptic clue. An example from The Times: "Great banana summit?"; solution "It must be an anagram" (which is an anagram of "great banana summit"!)

The puzzles in newspapers such as *The Times*, *Guardian* and *Telegraph* are easiest on Monday and get progressively harder throughout the week.

72

Play Darts

If you're competitive, think about improving your darts play at home so you can impress at the local watering hole. Here's how to get started if you need to set up from scratch.

⊙ Steps

1. Hang the dartboard so that the centre is 1.73 m (5 ft 8 in) from the floor.

2. Mark the throwing line, or "oche" (rhymes with "hockey"), with nonskid tape. The line should be 2.37 m (7 ft 9¼ in) from the face of the dartboard (not the wall), according to the World Darts Federation.

3. Make sure the tape mark lies so that the front edge is the actual line. In other words, a player may step on the tape, but not past it.

4. Give each player or team three darts, and determine who throws first by having each player or team representative throw one dart. The player or team whose dart is closest to the bull's-eye gets to go first.

5. Warm up, as competitive darts players do, by alternating throws until each person has thrown nine darts.

6. Once the game begins, take your turn by throwing your three darts.

7. Start from 301 and count downwards, subtracting each score from the total. The first player or team to reach exactly zero wins.

✳ Tip

For an alternative game of darts, throw five sets of three darts for each player and tot up the total scored. The highest scorer wins.

⚠ Warning

Resist the temptation to hang your dartboard on the back of a door, unless the door is kept permanently locked.

Play Marbles

Although most of us think of marbles as an old-fashioned pastime, the game is still fun for children of all ages and is played around the globe.

Steps

1. Draw a circle about 1 m (3 ft) wide. Use chalk on asphalt or concrete, a stick on earth, or a string on carpet or tile.

2. Select your shooter and place any marbles you wish to play with as targets inside the circle; the other players do the same. Shooters are designated marbles used to knock targets out of the ring. Your shooter should be larger than the other marbles so it's powerful enough to do its job. It should also look different from other marbles so you can distinguish it from them easily.

3. Take your turn when the time comes by shooting your marble from outside the ring at any marble or marbles inside the ring. Shoot by kneeling on the ground and flicking your marble out of your fist with your thumb.

4. Gather any marbles you've knocked out of the ring.

5. Shoot again if you knocked any marbles out of the ring. Let the next player shoot if you haven't knocked any marbles out and/or your shooter remains in the ring.

6. Continue shooting in turn until the ring is empty.

7. Count your marbles at the end of the game. The winner is the player with the most marbles.

8. Return the marbles to their original owners unless you're playing "keepsies". In that case, each player keeps the marbles he or she won during the game.

Tips

These are the rules for a version of "ring taw" marbles, an older, more common variant. There are many other ways to play.

One way to decide playing order is called "lagging". The players line up opposite a line 3 m (10 ft) away (the "lag line") and shoot their marbles at it. The player whose marble ends up closest to the line goes first, the next closest goes second, and so on.

74

Juggle

Juggling is a matter of learning to catch and throw at the same time. Work up from one ball to two balls to three balls.

⊙ Steps

1 Hold a ball in your right hand.

2 Be aware that as you juggle, you'll be moving your hands in two independent circles – your right hand clockwise and your left hand anti-clockwise. The left hand lags about half a rotation.

3 Throw the ball with your right hand so that the apex – the highest point – of its path is about head-high.

4 Catch the ball as it drops into your left hand, then throw it up again, catching it with your right hand. Practise this manoeuvre until you go blind with boredom.

5 Proceed with a ball in each hand and continue as you did with one ball, throwing the second ball just as the first reaches its apex, and catching each ball with the other hand.

6 Practise with two balls until you feel confident. Try starting with the left hand once you've mastered starting with the right.

7 Add a third ball by starting with two balls in your right hand and one ball in your left hand.

8 Begin as you did with two balls, by throwing one of the balls from your right hand and then throwing the ball from your left hand when the first ball reaches its apex.

9 Catch the first ball with your left hand.

10 Throw the third ball (from your right hand) when the second ball reaches its apex.

11 Catch the second ball in your right hand.

Fun Activities

12 Throw the first ball from your left hand as the third ball reaches its apex.

13 Catch the third ball in your left hand.

14 Keep throwing each ball just as the ball thrown from the opposite hand reaches its apex. You will always have at least one ball in the air, and you will never have more than one ball in either hand.

 Tips

Juggle facing a wall to keep the balls from running away from you. Also, try juggling things that don't bounce – such as bean bags – so you don't have to chase after them.

Stand over your bed or sofa while juggling so you don't have to bend down as far to retrieve dropped balls.

If you're having trouble reacting quickly enough, try throwing the balls higher to give yourself more time to catch them.

75

Walk on Stilts

Stilt-walking is an ancient art that only requires a pair of stilts, optional protective padding and lots of practice. Soon you'll be able to view the world from a whole new perspective.

Steps

1 Begin with a low pair of stilts that places your feet about 30 cm (1 ft) off the ground. If you're concerned about injuring yourself in a fall, you might also want to wear a helmet and protective padding on your knees, elbows and wrists.

2 Select a firm, even surface on which to walk – the stilts could sink into softer ground, making them difficult to manoeuvre. Also, try to position yourself next to a wall that you can use as support, or between two low surfaces that you can use to prop yourself up, the way a gymnast uses parallel bars.

3 Make sure you have someone to "spot" (or catch) you who can handle your entire weight. Alternatively, string a rope tightly across your

training area at the level where your hands will be when you're on stilts. Use this for support and balance.

4　Grasp one stilt in each hand, set one foot on the little ledge sticking out from one stilt, and straighten your leg. Have your spotter prop you up if need be.

5　Once the first stilt feels secure, raise your other foot on to the second stilt and straighten this leg.

6　Practise stepping on the spot to get a feel for lifting your legs with the stilts properly. Begin walking only after you feel comfortable taking steps.

7　Take your first step forwards and then keep moving – it's easier to keep your balance that way.

8　Pretend you're marching – picking up each stilt high as you walk – so you don't trip on bumps on the ground.

9　Practise until you feel comfortable.

10　Progress to taller stilts as you feel ready.

✳ Tips

Learn how to fall correctly. You want to curve yourself inwards a little and try to land on a wide part of your body, such as your shoulders, which can better absorb the impact.

Take slow, small steps in the beginning to avoid "the splits".

76
Skip Stones

Nothing accompanies deep thought better than skipping stones across a body of water.

◎ Steps

1　Select a stone that's round, flat and smooth.

2　Stand at the edge of a large, placid body of water.

3　Hold the stone horizontally – flat side down – with your index finger curling around one edge.

Fun Activities

4   Aim the stone, ensuring there is no one near your line of fire.

5   Throw the stone low and parallel to the water's surface. Throw sidearm so that your hand travels past your waist and the stone travels horizontally across the water.

6   Release the stone with a snap of the wrist to give it a horizontal spin. Your elbow will be next to your hip as the stone leaves your hand.

7   Count the number of times the stone skips.

✳ Tips

The harder you throw the stone, the higher it may ricochet after the first skip. Three or more skips is very good. Eight is extraordinary. More than 12 is mythical.

You want the flat part of the rock to skip along the water's smooth surface.

77

Make a Paper Aeroplane

You don't need to be a pilot to get an old-fashioned introduction to aviation. Grab a piece of paper and start flying jets in your own back garden.

Steps

1   Find a rectangular-shaped piece of paper. A sheet of A4 copier paper is a good size and weight.

2   Lay the paper on a table with one of the long edges closest to you.

3   Fold the paper in half lengthwise. When the two edges match up, use your thumbs to make a sharp crease along the fold.

4   Take the upper left corner of the top layer of paper and fold it diagonally down towards the first crease you made. When the edges match up, use your thumbs to make a sharp crease along the new fold, which should create a small triangular flap.

5   Turn the paper over.

6   Take the upper right corner of the top layer of paper and fold it diagonally towards you, until the edge lines up with the first crease

you made. When the edges match, make a sharp crease along the new fold. (This is a mirror of what you did in step 4.)

7　Take the newly formed diagonal edge on the right side of the paper, and fold it straight down towards the first crease you made. When the edges match, make another sharp crease.

8　Turn the paper over, and again fold the diagonal edge down towards the first crease you made; make another sharp crease.

9　Form the wings by flipping the airplane over and repeating steps 7 and 8.

10　Hold the paper in one hand along the first crease you made. Let the wings of the plane flare out.

11　At a point about 20 cm (4 in) from the nose of the plane, make a 1.3 cm (½ in) rip in the bottom part of the plane; make another rip 1.3 cm (½ in) behind it. Fold this tab up.

12　Hold the aeroplane near the tab and toss the plane with an overhand, horizontal forward motion.

✳ Tips

Experiment with the size and weight of the paper.

Experiment with the location of the tab.

Make sharp creases to ensure a good flight.

78

Fly a Kite

A windy day in the park might keep you from flying a paper aeroplane outdoors, but it could be the perfect day to practise launching a kite.

◎ Steps

1　Check your local weather report to see if conditions are favourable for kite flying. Look for light to moderate winds if you're a beginner at kite flying, or gustier winds if you are more experienced. A wind speed of 8-24 kph (5-15 mph) is best for kite flying.

2. Find a large and windy open area free of trees and power lines – two things that are notoriously dangerous for kites and their owners.

3. Hold the kite in both hands and toss it lightly into the wind until the wind catches it. This works well when the wind is moderately strong.

4. Alternatively, let out a small length of kite string and, holding the string in your hand, run with the kite behind you until the wind lifts it.

5. Begin letting out string until the kite reaches a height with which you are comfortable. Good heights range from 15 to 30 m (50 to 100 ft).

6. Keep an eye on your kite, as it may come crashing down because of sudden changes in wind. If it dips, run or pull in the string a bit to give it some lift.

7. Bring the kite down by slowly winding the kite string around a kite spool.

8. Reach out and grab the kite before it hits the ground to avoid damaging it.

✳ Tips

Tighten the string around a spool and secure the spool to the ground if you want to tend to other activities.

Tie additional ribbon or strips of cloth to the tail to increase the stability of diamond kites in gusty winds.

⚠ Warning

Stay away from electricity power lines! If a kite becomes entangled, leave it there. And never fly your kite during a thunderstorm.

79

Teach Your Parrot to Talk

As satisfied bird owners can attest, teaching a parrot to talk takes patience but is well worth the effort.

◎ Steps

1. Begin teaching your parrot to talk when she is 4 to 6 months old at the latest. Try a simple "Good morning" to your bird at the start of

each day. Keep in mind that some parrots will pick up words sooner than others.

2 Hold the bird in front of your mouth when you teach her, so that you have her attention.

3 Repeat words or phrases, such as family members' names and common expressions. Be sure to show lots of excitement in your voice. Your parrot will gradually begin to repeat after you.

4 Repeat certain words or phrases every time you do something, such as "Up" when you lift your bird up, to teach her to associate a particular movement with certain words.

5 Reward with treats when your parrot mimics you.

6 Consider playing recordings of words you want her to learn for up to 15 minutes at a time – longer than that can cause boredom.

 Tips

Don't let your bird hear sounds or words you don't want her to mimic. Discourage unwanted utterances by simply ignoring them.

Some experts believe that parrot owners should teach their birds to talk before teaching them to whistle, as whistling can interfere with learning words.

Mynah birds and certain types of parakeets can also learn to repeat words.

80

Be Happy

Happiness has different meanings for everyone; we each have to define and seek it for ourselves.

⊙ Steps

1 Decide what is important to you in life. For example: Do you value a certain kind of job; material things; a relationship; time alone or with others; time to relax or to be creative; time to read, listen to music or have fun? These are just a few of the possibilities.

Relationships

2   Think about times when you have felt happy, good, or content. Where were you? Whom were you with? What were you doing, thinking or experiencing that made you feel happy?

3   Decide to make more time in your life to do more of what is important to you and makes you feel happier. To be happy, you have to make happiness a priority in your life.

4   Start with little things and work up to bigger ones. Little things might include reading an engrossing book for 15 minutes; taking a walk; telephoning a friend; or buying scented soap, shampoo, candles or tea that you will enjoy every time you use them.

5   Focus on what is positive about yourself, others and life in general instead of dwelling on the negative. Write down as many positive things as you can think of in a journal. Keep it handy to read over and continue adding to it.

6   Appreciate what is working in your life at the moment. In the major areas of your life, such as your health, job, love life, friends, family, money and living situation, what is going well?

✳ Tips

Ask other people, "What makes you happy?" or "What is something that makes you feel good?"

It's OK to ask for professional help. Talk to someone, such as a psychotherapist, career counsellor or spiritual adviser (minister or teacher) to help you sort out what would make you happy.

Read books on the subject of happiness. Wise people have been writing about it for hundreds of years. In the bookshop, look under psychology, spirituality, or philosophy.

81

Overcome Shyness

Everyone feels shy sometimes, but being too shy can hamper many aspects of your life.

Steps

1   Determine why you're shy in the first place. For example, are you afraid of what someone might say about your physical appearance?

Remember, there's an underlying reason for how you react in situations.

2 Act as if you're not shy. In private, behave as if you're oozing confidence. Hold your chin up, stand up straight and tall, stride confidently and speak firmly. It may seem ridiculous, but you will see results when you're out in public.

3 Practise making eye contact and smiling when you have interactions with others. Strike up casual conversations with strangers about the weather or current events.

4 Look your best. One way to reduce self-consciousness is to always look good and limit opportunities for being self-critical.

5 Decrease your fear of rejection by imagining the worst possible outcome. If you approach someone, he or she may say no to your overture or may just walk away. Everybody has been rejected at some point, but no one has to dwell on it.

6 Look and learn. Watching friends or even strangers who aren't shy is a good way to learn some tips first-hand.

7 Develop a positive feeling about yourself, don't get frustrated, and have fun. Keep in mind that the real goal is to meet people who will like you for who you are.

 Tip

Find out about progressive relaxation techniques. These same steps can be applied to situations that cause you to feel shy.

82

Find the Best Places to Meet People

Still looking for the man or woman of your dreams? If you're wasting hours on end hanging out at the corner bar or the local gym, you might want to change your strategy.

Relationships

1. Choose a place that interests you. This increases your chances of meeting people who are interested in similar things.

2. Be creative about where you go. Parties and other social gatherings are the most obvious places to make new acquaintances, but don't leave out other options, such as club meetings and classes.

3. Go academic: college and university are great places to meet people. Why not sign up for a summer school or evening classes.

4. Mingle: parties, dances and cinema queues are fun places to meet people who make an effort to go out.

5. Don't overlook opportunities in public places: supermarkets, launderettes, bookshops, cafés and restaurants are all casual spots to meet new people.

6. Ask around – friends and relatives are good sources for helping you meet other people.

7. Look around locally. Proximity plays a big part in friendships as well as romantic relationships, and you may find that the special someone you seek is right around the corner.

8. Look in your community. Familiar places like your church, synagogue or mosque are good venues for seeing who's out there.

9. Use the newspaper. Place a personal ad or respond to one.

10. Try meeting people online. There are numerous websites that feature chat rooms, personal ads and individual photos.

⚠ Warnings

If you meet a potential romantic partner at work, think carefully before proceeding – is it worth the possible complications?

Try not to seem desperate – people may find this unattractive.

Flirt

Not a natural flirt? Don't worry – anyone can learn the basic social skills that will attract others.

◉ Steps

1　Be confident – it's the magical charm that makes others want to get to know you.

2　Smile, smile, smile.

3　Think playful thoughts when gearing up to flirt. Flirts are fun and engaging, and they love to play with others.

4　Compliment a stranger or acquaintance on his or her clothes, eyes, smile or sense of humour, for starters.

5　Keep your body language open and inviting: make eye contact, lightly touch the person's hand or arm when telling a story, toss your head back when you laugh.

6　Initiate stimulating conversation. At a loss for words? Ask open-ended questions about the flirtee's job, home town, family, recent films seen or thoughts about a painting on the wall.

7　Open up about yourself, giving someone even more reason to like you. But don't go on and on – the goal is to engage and intrigue, not bore.

8　Gauge the person's interest carefully. If you sense a red light – or worse, smug ridicule – make your exit graciously and immediately. You've got nicer people to meet.

9　Progress in your flirtation, paying attention to cues from the object of your interest. If you perceive a sensual or sexual connection, make a bold move – ask for a date.

✳ Tips

Avoid negative body language, such as crossing your arms, scowling, appearing overly stressed, looking downwards or walking in a hurry when you don't really need to.

Give yourself time to learn the types of conversation starters that work

for you. Practise flirting wherever you can – at the local shop or launderette, or with your friends.

⚠ Warning

Sexually suggestive remarks or touching is inappropriate among colleagues. Keep any office flirting innocent at all times.

84
Survive the Bar Scene

You agreed to go out with your friends to a bar or club. Instead of dwelling on how you allowed such a thing to happen, have fun by following these simple tips.

⊙ Steps

1. Enjoy yourself, first and foremost. Would you rather be at home washing the dishes? If the answer is yes, keep thinking of mundane chores until you find one you would not want to be doing at the moment.

2. You see someone you think you'd like to know better. He or she ignores you. So? Pat yourself on the back for knowing that your soul mate is not necessarily hanging out in a meat market. Let it go and find someone else with better manners.

3. Be someone you're not – try on a new hat. Play the part of the spoiled rich girl, the alpha-wolf guy, the dumb blonde.

4. Be careful not to drink too much, in case you are approached by someone with a bad pick-up line. "May I end this sentence with a proposition?" might work on you if you have had a few too many.

5. Remember, though, that as lame as pick-up lines might be, the person is making an effort to show an interest in you. If you are even remotely interested, laugh, say hello and begin a normal conversation.

6. Be polite if someone wants to talk to you and you aren't interested. If the person won't leave you alone, say that you have a boyfriend or girlfriend.

7. Save your flirting for when you really want to use it.

Be sure you know how you're getting home before you go out.

Interestingly enough, 71 per cent of men report success when they use the pickup line "Hi".

⚠️ Warning

Don't put yourself into a dangerous situation, such as being alone in a dark alley with a strange man – or woman.

85

↑ ↑ ↑

Make Small Talk

Small talk can be a big challenge, but preparation and confidence are all you really need.

◎ Steps

1   Practise. Converse with everyone you encounter: cashiers, waiters, people you're in a queue with, neighbours, co-workers, and kids. Chat with people unlike yourself, from the elderly to teenagers to tourists.

2   Read everything: cookbooks, newspapers, magazines, reviews, product inserts, maps, signs and catalogues. Everything is a source of information that can be turned into interesting conversations.

3   Force yourself to get into small-talk situations, such as doctors' waiting rooms, cocktail parties, and meetings at the office. Accept invitations or host your own gathering.

4   Immerse yourself in culture, both high and low. Television, music, sports, fashion, art and poetry are great sources of chat. If you can't stand Shakespeare, your dislike of the bard is also a good topic for discussion.

5   Keep a diary. Write down funny stories you hear, beautiful things you see, quotes, observations, shopping lists, and phone calls you made. That story about the time when the man at the call centre misunderstood you could become an opening line.

6   Talk to yourself in the mirror. Make a random list of topics and see

Relationships

what you have to say on the subjects. Tennis, Russia, butter, hip-hop, shoes – the more varied your list, the better.

7 Expand your horizons. Go home a new way. Try sushi. Play pinball. Go online. Paint a watercolour. Bake a pie. Try something new every day.

8 Be a better listener. Did your boss say that she suffers from migraines? Has your doctor just had twins? These are opportunities for making small talk.

9 Work on building up your confidence, overcoming shyness and banishing any feelings of stage fright. Remember, the more you know, the more you know you can talk about.

 ## Tips

Be yourself. Confidence and uniqueness are superb substitutes for comedic genius.

Keep a few exit lines in mind. For example, "Thanks for the wonderful conversation, but now I have to give the impression I'm interested in everybody else."

⚠ Warning

Keep your fellow chatterers in mind; naughty stories and loose language will be frowned upon in many circles. Similarly, your French quips and scientific discourses will be wasted on some.

86
Know if Someone Is Lying

There are often cues and signs that a person may be lying. But there may also be understandable reasons for the lie.

⊚ Steps

1 Look for body language that might indicate someone is lying, such as not looking you in the eye when speaking to you, being fidgety, or seeming nervous or uncomfortable.

2 Listen for inconsistencies in what the person tells you, such as different stories on different days, different time frames, mistakes in remembering details or mixing up details.

3   Notice if the person steadfastly resists answering any of your questions. Extreme defensiveness could mean that he or she is hiding something.

4   Notice if the person accuses you of lying or being deceitful when you haven't been. This could reflect the accuser's own underlying behaviour, which he or she is projecting onto you rather than owning up to.

5   Listen to your gut reaction, or intuition. You may just know someone is lying. If you are not sure, don't jump to conclusions. Try to get some evidence to back up your hunch.

6   Consider asking directly if the person has lied to you. Many people feel guilty if they are caught lying and find it a relief to finally be honest.

7   Try to be understanding and listen to the person's reasons for lying. Was he trying not to hurt you? Was she afraid you would be angry or upset?

8   Look at your possible role in the situation. Are you someone who gets so upset hearing the truth that others feel they can't be honest with you?

⚠ Warning

Try not to assume that someone is lying unless your evidence is solid. Body language and intuition can provide clues but not proof.

87

Compliment a Man Who Catches Your Eye

A cute guy has just entered the café. What do you do? A straightforward compliment can lead to a beautiful friendship – or at least brighten his day.

◎ Steps

1   Be sincere and friendly; compliment him in the same way you would want to be complimented.

Relationships

2　Smile at him as he walks by. Giving special attention and obvious appreciation might be all you need to do.

3　Mention that he has a nice smile – but don't be lecherous. Simply say, "You've got a nice smile."

4　Note an attractive part of his outfit: "Like your shades!" "Cool sweater!"

5　Don't ogle.

6　Keep your appreciation of his Adonis-like features or body to yourself – anything you say about his physique will probably sound cheesy.

7　Give him credit for his pluck and originality if he sports a magenta, green or blue hairdo.

8　Compliment him in the context of the situation at hand. For example, tell him you admire his taste in reading material.

 Tip

Try not to be too extravagant, for example, saying you love something of his. Simple, straightforward compliments are best and leave little room for misinterpretation.

⚠ Warning

Use compliments sparingly lest you appear insincere.

88

Compliment a Woman Who Catches Your Eye

You spot an intriguing woman and must establish contact or live with regret for the rest of the day. How do you compliment her without appearing too aggressive? Or, worse, tasteless?

◎ Steps

1　Think about commenting on actions over looks: "Great moves!" for the groover on the dance floor, or "Healthy diet!" for the good-looking woman buying greens at the supermarket.

2   Commend a woman for her wit or intelligence ("Funny joke!" "Great idea!") rather than her beautiful breasts.

3   Compliment a woman's appearance – hair, clothes, jewellery – only if you can do so with a sincere smile, or she'll think you're giving her a line and you might get a frosty response.

4   Consider compliments that may lead to conversation: "Love your car – how do you find it to drive?"

5   Consider asking her first if she likes receiving compliments. If she smiles encouragingly, tell her she's got a great smile; if she gives you a dirty look, just look the other way.

6   Get creative. If a woman has unbelievable violet eyes or an extraordinary and exotic name, she's probably used to getting compliments about these unusual features. Compliment her on something less obvious – she'll appreciate that you noticed what others usually don't.

✳ Tip

Watch out for half-compliments that could do more damage than good: "You're going to look so beautiful when you finally get your braces taken off."

⚠ Warning

Avoid sarcasm and smirking when you give compliments, especially if those behavioural no-nos tend to occur when you're nervous.

89

Know if Someone Likes You Romantically

Sometimes the direct approach is best – just ask. But if that seems too bold, look for some of these telling signs.

◎ **Steps**

Behaviour

1   Pay attention to your conversations with the person in question. Does this person show a special interest in talking with you and, once it's started, make an effort to keep that conversation going?

Relationships

2. Does this person "accidentally" run into you in places where he knows you will be, such as at your desk? At the launderette on Tuesdays? At your brother's birthday party?

3. Notice whether this person mentions future plans to spend time with you: "That band is coming here soon. We should really get tickets."

4. Notice if the person is making an effort to spend time alone together. Cancelling other plans in order to be with you longer, or finding excuses not to leave, could be a sign of romantic interest.

5. Has the person been calling for seemingly random reasons, such as, "I was wondering if you knew what that pizza place down the street is called", followed by, "Are you hungry?"

6. Has the person taken a sudden interest in your life and hobbies? This is a sure sign that she is interested in something – and it's probably not your stamp collection.

7. Observe how the person acts around your friends – he might be extra friendly to your closest pals for a reason.

Body Language

1. Sometimes seeing someone you have a crush on results in telltale physiological signs. Does the person in question blush when you look at her? Her sympathetic nervous system is probably going into overdrive. Does she jumble her words when talking to you?

2. See if the person mirrors your movements: when you lean back, he leans back; when you put your elbows on the table, he does the same.

3. Notice whether this person sits or stands in the open position – that is, facing you with arms uncrossed, or crossing her legs in your direction if the person is a woman.

4. Does he move closer to you and/or touch you subtly, such as patting your hand or touching your cheek?

5. Look for other elements of body language, such as frequent eye contact, holding your gaze and looking down before looking away, energetic speech coupled with open hands, or flashing palms.

6. Does the person you're wondering about smile at you a lot?

Trust in your intuition and listen to your feelings.

Feel flattered if a friend or co-worker likes you romantically, but don't view it as a personal crisis if you can't return the affections. Your admirer will probably move on once you make it clear that you don't feel the same way.

90

Ask for a Phone Number

Say you're at the supermarket and out of nowhere comes your dream mate. Don't just stand there speechless in aisle 9 – ask for a phone number!

⊙ Steps

1 Approach the person. Remember that eye contact and a gentle smile are crucial in appearing friendly.

2 Enter the conversation with a compliment, then introduce yourself. Try not to be too cute with your delivery; sincerity usually goes down better than an elaborate pick-up line.

3 Talk. You'll get a strong sense of whether the person would be willing to give you a phone number. If no eye contact or smile is coming your way, and you're making a solid effort, then maybe you should give up.

4 Ask for the number if you're getting positive signals. Try not to be pushy, and show respect for the person's private information. Avoid "How about giving me your number?" Instead, use: "It would be great to get to know you better. Is there a number where I can reach you?"

5 Offer your own phone number after getting the other person's, if you feel comfortable doing so. Some women are not comfortable giving out their number, so if a woman declines to give you hers, you may still want to offer your own.

Opt for a person's work number if he or she appears uncomfortable with giving you a home number.

If you get a phone number, wait two days before calling so as not to appear desperate. Avoid waiting too long, though; he or she may forget about you.

91

Ask Someone on a Date

You'll never know whether the other person is interested unless you ask. So gather up all your courage and follow these steps.

Steps

1. Introduce yourself to that person you've been admiring from afar.

2. Ask for the person's telephone number, or tell a common friend that you would like the number.

3. Call at a time that's not intrusive. Make the call when you feel comfortable, regardless of what your friends might say about romantic protocol.

4. Reintroduce yourself once you're on the phone by saying something like, "Hi, it's Emma. We met at the art gallery."

5. Using as little pretence as possible (ideally none), ask the person if he or she would like to meet for a cup of coffee or do something similarly informal. If you are politely refused, take the hint and get off the phone.

6. Arrange to get together casually for a brief time – half an hour or so. If that goes well, suggest a more formal date, such as lunch.

Tips

Some of the best ideas for a date are the things you love to do the most, such as going to an art museum or getting muddy on a mountain bike ride.

If your invitation is rejected, congratulate yourself for trying and move on.

Going to see a film may not be ideal for a first date; it shows a lack of creativity and does not allow the two of you to spend much time talking.

92

Plan a Date on a Budget

You don't need to blow your bank account or rack up debt on your credit card to plan a fantastic date. All you need is a little imagination and the following pointers.

◎ Steps

1   Determine how much you can spend and the types of things you and your date might enjoy doing together.

2   Opt for the less expensive meet-at-a-café date or the drink-after-work date for a blind date, or if you don't yet know your mutual interests.

3   Consider an afternoon bike ride or walk through the park, or simply sitting by the river watching the boats go by.

4   Plan an evening picnic in the park, weather permitting. Coordinate with a free outdoor musical or play, and pack a bottle of wine, together with bread and cheese.

5   Consider inviting your date to a party; make any necessary introductions to your friends, have fun, then leave together after a relatively short time and go for a drink.

6   Try cooking dinner and renting a film. (This may or may not be an appropriate first date.)

 Tip

Ask the person to lunch and a matinee at the weekend – the inexpensive version of a Saturday-night dinner-and-a-film date.

Relationships

⚠ Warning

Avoid pretending you have money when you don't. But don't draw attention to the fact that you have little to spend – financial distress is never a turn-on.

93

Refuse a Date to Ensure No More Requests

Unless you want to be asked out again by this person, be direct and leave no room for misinterpretation.

⊙ Steps

1 Be clear, consistent and gracious in your refusal. Be politely neutral rather than emphatic.

2 Don't hesitate, procrastinate or ask to think about it.

3 Express regret, if you'd like, but never say anything you don't mean, such as, "Maybe another time."

4 Devise an impersonal, generic explanation if you prefer, such as, "I never date colleagues" or "I'm involved with someone else." Otherwise, simply refuse the invitation with a polite "Thank you for thinking of me. I'm sorry, I'll have to say no."

✳ Tip

If a person persists in asking you out, just persist in being firm and clear. Sooner or later, you'll get the message across.

Refuse a Date to Ensure Another Request

Sometimes circumstances are beyond your control. Here's how to refuse a date when you truly wish you could accept.

⊙ Steps

1. Smile and make eye contact if the invitation is made in person.

2. Communicate your complete attention if the request is made by phone. Consider saying something like "Excuse me while I close the door" or "I was hoping you'd call."

3. Express your thanks in whatever style is genuine and comfortable for you – a joke, a simple thanks, a great big "Wow!"

4. Communicate your regret at having to refuse, and explain why you need to decline the invitation.

5. Suggest another specific day, or express your general wish to find another time that works for both of you. A straightforward "I can't this time because I have to go to Glasgow, but I would love to make it another time. How about next Friday?" has candour to recommend it.

✱ Tips

People look for acceptance, so be open and enthusiastic.

If you simply say that you can't make it, the person may interpret that as a brush-off. Always provide an explanation.

Be clear, candid and gracious.

⚠ Warning

Asking someone out can be difficult, so make it as easy as possible for the other person.

Cancel a Date at the Last Minute

You've changed your mind about the date – or life has simply got in the way. How do you cancel at the last minute?

Steps

If You Want to Be Asked Out Again

1 Call as soon as possible. It's not likely you'll be forgiven easily if you let your date show up and wait for you, just to have you cancel.

2 Blame it on outside circumstances: an unexpected meeting, deadline or assignment. You really, really want to go, but ...

3 Tell the truth: you're tired, you don't feel well, you've had a rotten day. You'd rather stay in and rest than go out and not be very much fun.

4 Create an excuse: you forgot that you were meeting your friends for dinner, you need to go to your grandmother's to move her furniture, you lost your keys and can't leave until you find them.

5 Leave the conversation open for another invitation.

6 Suggest an alternative date.

7 Offer to make it up to him or her – and then do it. Send a card or a bouquet of flowers.

8 If your date calls later to check up on you, be where you said you'd be and thank him or her for being thoughtful.

If You Don't Want to Be Asked Out Again

1 Call as soon as you realise you want to cancel. Keep in mind how much easier cancelling is on the phone than in person.

2 Blame it on outside circumstances. Believable: you are really busy at work and don't have time for dating. Unbelievable: your power has been shut off so you haven't had a shower in four days.

3 Tell the truth: you're not interested; you've had a revelation that he or she is not The One.

4 Tell a white lie: you're seeing someone else, or you've decided that you don't want to date anyone just now.

5   Stay on the phone only long enough to deliver your message; be careful not to give the impression that you are interested.

 Tip

If you don't want another date, keep the conversation short. Don't apologise for not wanting to go out with this person. Ever.

96

Create a Romantic Atmosphere

When planning an intimate dinner or other event, use your imagination and ingenuity to arouse the senses with beautiful sights, sounds, flavours and aromas.

◎ Steps

Indoors

1   Set the mood by playing some soft, romantic music. Classical music is usually a safe bet, as are jazz and soul.

2   Fill the room with a dramatic array of flowers to add visual interest as well as inexpensive elegance.

3   Light the room with either bright, slow-burning candles or, if possible, the glow from a fireplace to add a warm, intimate tone to the evening.

4   Plan and prepare a simple yet elegant meal. Try to find out beforehand which foods your date particularly enjoys and serve them.

5   Include classic romantic fare, such as champagne and strawberries.

6   Use your best china, and select table linens and napkins in soft and sumptuous fabrics. If chosen well, these items can be purchased for little money but appear stylish and sophisticated, giving your date the impression that you've gone all out for the occasion.

Outdoors

1   Coordinate your plans with seasonal or natural events, such as a sunset, a full moon or the turning of the leaves during the autumn.

Relationships

2   Plan and prepare a simple yet elegant meal. If possible, include your date's favourite foods. Don't forget the wine or champagne.

3   Pack the meal and the necessary utensils in a picnic basket. Again, use the best china you have.

4   Bring along a picnic blanket as well as a big, soft blanket for warmth, should the night turn cold.

5   Bring along some candles or torches to provide light and warmth. Citronella candles are especially handy for warding off insects.

✳ Tips

Flowers are a staple of romance – use them liberally.

When planning an outdoor event, be sure to check the weather forecast and have an alternative plan in mind, just in case.

Things You'll Need

❏ music

❏ flowers

❏ candles

❏ romantic food and drink

❏ china

❏ table linen and napkins

97

Keep a Dozen Red Roses Fresh

To make that special and romantic gift last as long as possible, follow these guidelines.

◎ Steps

1   Store the roses in a cool place – ideally a refrigerator – if you can't get them into water immediately. A cool environment will help to slow the deterioration process.

2   Fill a vase with warm or tepid water. Make sure it's no cooler than room temperature. Warm water will be absorbed more quickly.

3   Add floral preservatives to the water if you have some available. Follow the package instructions.

4   Cut off any foliage that will lie below the waterline (it will rot), as well as any torn leaves.

5   Cut off about 2.5 cm (1 in) of the stems, either straight across or at a slant, using a knife rather than scissors. Do this while the stem is submerged in a basin of warm or tepid water.

6   Place the roses in water immediately after cutting them.

7   Change the water and recut the stems daily, taking extra care to remove any leaves that may have wilted or dipped into the water. This will help prevent bacteria build-up. If you're using preservatives, add more solution every other day.

8   Keep the flowers in a cool, dry place, away from direct sunlight, heaters, air conditioners and draughts. At night, move your roses to the coolest part of the house. This will help them last longer.

❋ Tips

There are many other factors that go into the duration of a cut rose, including rose type, gardening methods and climate; however, following these steps will allow you to keep your roses fresh for as long as possible.

You can make your own floral preservative using a citrus-based soft drink. Add one part soft drink for every three parts water.

98

Make a Great First Impression on a Date

Want to make sure your date will be eager to go out with you a second time? No problem.

◉ Steps

1   Dress attractively but comfortably. Don't wear clothes that make you feel stiff or self-conscious.

2   Be aware of your posture – it speaks volumes about you. You want to appear alert and confident by sitting up straight.

Relationships

3   Compliment your date. Don't just say "I like your shirt." Be sincere and notice something that he or she took time with.

4   Learn to flirt (see 517 "Flirt") and try it out. Don't overdo it, though.

5   Realise that you don't have to tell people how great you are. It's better to show them instead.

6   Be interested and interesting. Listen actively to what your date says. Ask questions and don't interrupt.

7   Enjoy yourself, no matter what. If you're easygoing and fun to be around, and if you can go with whatever comes your way, you can't help but make a great impression.

8   Thank the other person for the date – always, without exception. Good manners will get you far.

❉ Tips

Don't talk about anything negative or complain on a first date.

Be cautious about drinking – it will give you a false sense of confidence and your inhibitions will be lowered. You may say or do things you'll regret later.

99

Read Your Date's Body Language

Your date claims to be having fun, yet you catch him or her yawning uncontrollably. Body language says a lot about what your date is really thinking.

◎ Steps

Positive Body Language

1   Notice if your date's posture is good yet relaxed. A slouched date probably isn't having a good time. A date who's sitting up is paying attention.

2   Observe whether your date makes good eye contact. If he keeps looking into your eyes, you've got it made.

3   Is your date leaning forward? Then you aren't a stranger any more.

4   Be aware of any physical contact. Holding hands is a great sign.

5   Notice if your date has her palms up, which indicates a friendly warmth.

6   Know that your date is listening to you if he nods at appropriate times during the conversation; this indicates that your words are being heard.

7   Pay attention to whether your date is in sync with you and constantly reflecting your behaviour. Does she shift in her seat when you do? Does he pick up your speed and tone when he's speaking? This occurs unconsciously and indicates a good rhythm between you – it's not just a copycat game.

Negative Body Language

1   Take note if your date's arms are crossed. This suggests there's a wall between the two of you.

2   Beware if your date is yawning. This is a bad sign – unless it's because she was up all night thinking about you.

3   Notice if your date is nodding at inappropriate times or seems to be nodding constantly during your conversation. Your date may be thinking about something else.

4   Is your date looking at everything but you? Be worried.

5   Notice if your date is keeping some distance between you. Personal space is one thing, but if your date is not standing next to you when you're waiting in a cinema queue together, that's a bad sign.

✳ Tip

Interpreting body language isn't cut-and-dried; allow for the fact that your interpretation may be wrong.

⚠ Warning

Avoid pointing out your date's body language to him or her – this may put your date on the defensive.

Relationships

Kiss on a Date

The date's gone well, and now it's almost over. Here are some tips on the how and when of kissing.

Steps

1. Look for positive body language, such as eye contact, uncrossed arms and head tilted towards you.

2. Do it. Waiting just makes the moment awkward.

3. Maintain eye contact as you close in. Try not to close your eyes until after making lip contact.

4. Tilt your head slightly to one side to avoid bumping noses.

5. Press your lips gently against your date's. Try not to suck his or her breath away just yet.

6. Release. Look into your date's eyes. If he or she isn't looking back at you the same way, then you probably shouldn't continue.

7. Kiss your date again. There's more flexibility to this kiss.

8. Explore – softly kiss your date's neck, ears and eyelashes. By this time, you'll have a better feel for how and where to kiss your date.

Tip

Keep the kissing simple for now. Use a soft touch that will calm your date, especially if this kiss is the first one.

Decide Whether to Go on a Third Date

You made it past the first and second dates. Now it's time to decide: is this worth pursuing?

⊙ Steps

1. Assess the relationship. Who is making the plans? Is it both of you or just one of you? Are the decisions truly mutual?

2. How interested are you? You probably don't know each other very well yet, but are you beginning to feel comfortable with this person? Can you talk about some of your thoughts and feelings?

3. Does he or she seem interested in you?

4. Think about your shared interests. Do you have any of the same hobbies? Do you enjoy the same kinds of weekend activities?

5. Take note of your differences. Some can be a problem, while others may add interest. Do you have fun listening to his fishing stories, even though you'd never go yourself? That's a good sign. Are you put off by her vocal political opinions? Better forgo the third date.

6. Do your conversations keep getting more interesting? Or are you already running out of things to talk about?

7. Do you talk on the phone apart from setting up dates?

8. Have you seen any signs of psychological gamesmanship? If so, don't continue this unless you really enjoy the abuse.

9. Were you thanked on the first two dates? Regardless of who paid, it's nice to know that someone appreciated spending time with you.

10. How comfortable would you be meeting his or her parents? That may tell you a lot about how well you're clicking.

✳ Tips

If you decide to go on a third date, make sure to take it slow. Even though all the signs are looking positive, you need time to get to know each other better before getting serious.

If you decide against a third date, be firm and respectful in letting the other person know. Treat him or her the way you would like to be treated in this situation.

Know When It's Over

Is it time to call it quits?

Steps

1. Be realistic. If you're being abused, hurt, cheated on or lied to, it's time to cut your losses and get out.

2. Think about the future you're creating. If your partner is jealous, obsessive, possessive or overly emotional, consider the extra burden you are carrying in dealing with those behaviours.

3. Is he a shameless flirt? Is she bossy? demanding? insecure? These are more signs of a rocky road ahead.

4. Do you truly enjoy each other's company, or do you find yourself relieved whenever you part company? If the latter, it doesn't bode well.

5. Evaluate your role in maintaining the relationship. If it feels as though you're doing all the work, it's time to talk or walk.

6. Does he promise to call and then forget? Is she terminally late? Be honest with yourself. Is this what you want?

7. Do you feel accepted and appreciated? If not, move on.

Tip

Make sure you want to end the relationship because the person is wrong for you and not because you fear commitment. You don't want to send Prince Charming packing just because you have commitment jitters.

Break Up Peacefully

If you're ready to end a relationship, consider how you can break up without conflict.

◎ Steps

1. Acknowledge that the relationship is really over. Come to terms with your own feelings and make a firm decision to end the relationship.

2. Don't delay the inevitable. Once you decide to break up with your partner, immediately think about how, when and where you will take action.

3. Make sure you're the one who personally delivers the news. Don't give a third party the opportunity to tell your partner that you want to break up before you have the chance to discuss the matter alone.

4. Select a private place to meet your partner to end the relationship.

5. Find or schedule an appropriate time. Approach the topic when both of you are calm and rational. Don't announce your intention to break up during a heated argument or a moment of anger.

6. Show your resolve by being firm, decisive and honest. Help your partner understand why you want to end the relationship. Be tactful, not brutal.

7. Remind your partner that you'll never forget the positive qualities in your relationship, but emphasise that you're ready to move on with your life.

8. Give your partner the closure that he or she needs to accept the break-up; answer questions and talk it over instead of leaving loose ends.

9. Stay positive as you both make plans to go your separate ways.

✳ Tip

Let go of old grievances during a break-up. The end of a relationship isn't the appropriate time to bring up old grudges.

Relationships

If your partner does not agree to the break-up, don't allow him or her to manipulate you into staying in the relationship.

104

Handle a Break-Up

Whether you're the one doing the dumping or the one getting dumped, breaking up is always hard to do. Although you might feel as if you'll never get over this, you will.

◉ Steps

1. Call all your friends – even those you may have ignored during your recent relationship – and make plans immediately. Now is not a good time to be alone.

2. Vent emotion when the need arises. Good friends will let you take out the photo album (again) and cry (again) and rant (again) – and they'll still love you.

3. Allow yourself time to grieve. If you don't let yourself wallow in self-pity for a while and mourn the good times lost, your heart may harden to future relationships and love.

4. Realise that this sadness will pass.

5. Distract yourself with fun once you're tired of mourning. Films, group sports, classes or a favourite CD can help take your mind off your loss.

6. Indulge yourself when you're feeling lonely. Try a massage, a weekend trip away with a best friend, a great new outfit – whatever helps you feel good about yourself.

7. Begin dating again when you're ready. Let friends set you up, and go to all those parties you might otherwise skip.

8. Analyse what went wrong in the relationship only after you have rebuilt your self-esteem. If you attempt to do this too soon, you're headed for another downward spiral.

9   Remember the good aspects of the relationship (there must have been some), and then get excited about the new direction your life is suddenly taking. Change can be great!

 Tip

Keep in mind that clean breaks are generally better than those mini-breaks or sort-of break-ups that are a bit easier to deal with at the time. Upon breaking up, attempt to resolve lingering issues, then take some time away from each other, even if you intend to remain friends.

⚠ Warnings

Never sleep with an ex unless you like to torture yourself.

While you're upset, don't do anything you'll regret later. The transition back into single life is a highly vulnerable time. Get support from your friends.

105

Know if You're in Love

Determining if you're in love involves serious soul-searching.

◎ Steps

1   Clarify what love is for you. Write down all your thoughts and feelings about what a loving relationship would be like for you. Ask other people how they define love or know if they love someone.

2   Distinguish between love (as you've defined it) and lust or infatuation. Lust is an intense sexual desire. Infatuation refers to the initial stage of a relationship, when you are "mad" about your new love interest; this feeling usually fades over time.

3   Write down how you do feel about the person. For example: you enjoy his or her company, have similar interests, feel safe, trust the person, think he or she is attractive, and so on.

4   Think about how well the two of you relate to each other. For example, how well do you communicate with each other? How do you deal with conflict? Do you bring out good or bad parts of each other? Can you show different sides of yourself?

Relationships

5   Ask yourself if you see and accept your love interest as a whole
     person. True love isn't just about loving the parts of someone that are
     easy to appreciate, but choosing to love that person overall.

 Tips

Infatuation, when you may think you are in love and have found the
perfect person, lasts about six months. But it often takes more time to
tell if you are truly compatible and if you can love the whole person in
the longer term.

Read books on the subject of love. Wise people have been writing
about it for hundreds of years.

106
Say "I Love You"

Ready to take the plunge and introduce that most romantic
phrase into your relationship's dialogue?

Steps

1   Decide if you do, indeed, love your mate. Most partners can see
     through a halfhearted "love ya" – which won't do your relationship any
     good.

2   Consider the possibility that your partner might not respond with the
     hoped-for "I love you, too." If you can handle that and still want to
     express your love, go for it. If you can't, then consider holding off until
     either you're certain your partner will respond as hoped or you're OK
     with it if he or she doesn't.

3   Think about how you'd like to let your partner know the way you feel,
     keeping in mind that uttering those words may give birth to a lifelong
     memory. If spontaneity works for you, wait for the perfect moment. If
     you're more methodical, consider writing a love letter first, then telling
     your mate in person the next time you get together.

4   If you decide in advance when to reveal your love, plan a special
     evening around it. Such relationship milestones warrant celebration.

5   When you tell your partner you love him or her, do so while making total eye contact, and while you are holding each other. This gives the moment the intimacy it deserves.

 Tip

Avoid saying the "L" word for the first time in the heat of passion – your partner may doubt the sincerity of your proclamation.

107

Write a Love Letter

Here is how to profess everlasting love for your one and only in a proper love letter.

⊙ Steps

1   Select stationery appropriate to your personality and sentiment. Decide whether you prefer torn-out notebook paper, perfumed sheets covered with flowers, or elegant note cards.

2   Determine the letter's purpose. Are you writing to tell your longtime love that you miss him or her, or initiating contact with someone you don't know very well?

3   Date your letter for posterity's sake.

4   Begin with Dear, Dearest, Beloved, My Precious, or whatever endearment or salutation feels appropriate for the depth of your relationship.

5   Be sure to thank your lover if you're responding to a letter, and mention the number of times you've reread it. Flatter your lover by repeating a couple of choice phrases he or she used.

6   Describe how your loved one makes you feel. Try to be original, but put sincerity ahead of creativity. The purpose of the letter is to express your feelings, not to stun your partner with a brilliant metaphor.

7   Mention his or her adorable traits. Bring up specific qualities or idiosyncrasies you appreciate. Be sparing with references to eyes and smiles, which can seem forced or clichéd, and try not to get melodramatic.

8   Recall your past times together and describe your hopes for the future.

9   Close with an exhortation to write back quickly, a mention of the next time you expect to see each other, or another appropriate comment.

10 Affix a proper valediction – such as "Yours", "Love" or "Feverishly Awaiting Your Letter" – depending on how you feel.

11 Read your letter aloud to check for awkward or stilted phrasing.

12 Finish your letter or envelope with a wax seal. Consider affixing a flower to it or enclosing a poem.

❋ Tips

Handwrite the letter. Laser printing isn't very romantic.

Write a draft, set it aside briefly, then read it again. Tone the letter down if necessary.

Consider other creative means of expressing your devotion: scrawl confessions on a mirror, fan or piece of cloth. Fire off a quick succession of postcards.

108
Make a Long-Distance Relationship Last

Whoever first said that absence makes the heart grow fonder never contended with the weekend airport or train rush. Here are some ways to hold on to your long-distance lover – and your sanity.

◉ Steps

1   Keep in touch daily. If large phone bills are a concern, send e-mail, letters, cards and even faxes.

2   Plan reunions to keep both of you pleased about the relationship. If
    your partner needs closeness, set up plans to meet often. Having a
    date to look forward to can help you through the rough times.

3   Reaffirm your love and commitment to one another. Try not to assume
    that the relationship is thriving. Listen to your partner's concerns and
    communicate your own before they become bigger problems.

4   Keep your partner informed about your life. You may live separately,
    but sharing information about your activities and friends is still
    important.

5   Trust one another. Suspicion will only break the relationship down.

6   Keep the relationship a high priority. Avoid cancelling reunions or
    putting off a phone call.

7   Focus on the future. Make plans to live in the same city eventually.

 Tips

Plan a reunion in a city other than the ones you live in. Having a
weekend getaway or holiday together can help recharge the relationship
and reinforce your commitment.

Find ways to reduce the costs of travel and phone calls so you can meet
and talk more often.

Surprise your loved one with an unexpected visit or a bouquet of flowers
to keep the passion alive.

Be patient – it may take time for long-term plans to work out.

109

Know if You Will Marry Your Significant Other

Is the object of your affections the right one for you? Keep
your eyes open for signs that this is the person you want to
marry.

Relationships

1. Examine your conversations. Does your partner include you in her plans when she talks about the future?

2. Consider the compatibility of your activities and values. Are you interested in your loved one's work and hobbies? Does your partner seem to be interested in your job and pastimes, even if she doesn't share your passion for them?

3. Consider whether you're both travelling along the same pathway in life. Do you want the same things, such as kids, stability, money, career?

4. Evaluate how your partner treats you in private and in public. Does he brag about you? Does he seem proud to be with you, or does he avoid being seen with you in public? Does he stick around when you're having a bad day, or does he disappear when you need him the most?

5. Evaluate how your significant other treats your friends and family. Is she willing to be nice to them, even if she doesn't like them?

6. Assess your partner's honesty and trustworthiness. Does he do what he says he's going to do? Do you feel you can trust him?

7. Think about all the reasons why you really like this person. Remember that infatuation fades, but genuine compatibility endures.

8. Communicate with your partner and discuss these issues to figure out if you're meant for each other.

❄ Tip

If the person seems secretive or ashamed to be seen with you in public, reevaluate your relationship. He or she may be trying to hide something or someone from you.

Get Him to Propose

You've found the man of your dreams, and you know you're meant for each other, but he needs a little nudge. Here's how to point him in the right direction.

Steps

1 Make him aware of your interest in a lifetime commitment. Drop subtle hints from time to time, such as, "We'd make a great team" or "I can't imagine my future without you", rather than incessantly bombarding him with demands about marriage.

2 Point out your shared interests, values and common goals. Open his eyes so he'll realise that you're the one for him.

3 Remember that actions speak louder than words. Show him what a great lifetime partner you could be through thoughtful actions, sincerity, kindness and other appealing traits.

4 Create opportunities for him to pop the question. Plan a candlelight dinner, arrange a romantic evening out or have a weekend away together.

5 Remind him of several happily married couples who are mutual friends of yours, pointing out how much you have in common with them and how successful their marriages are.

6 Express your happiness, love and devotion to him. Show him by your actions and words that you've found the man of your dreams – and you're ready to marry him!

Tip

Make sure not to fixate on this issue, as it may have a detrimental effect on the relationship. Give him the time he needs to sort things out.

Relationships

Propose Marriage to a Man

You're not the type of girl to wait around for Prince Charming.
You know what you want, so why not ask for it? Here are
some thoughts on how to propose to the man in your life.

Steps

1. Know your beloved well and anticipate his response. Will he be swept
   away by this romantic gesture? Or could he feel threatened by a
   woman's proposing marriage? (If so, you may want to reconsider.)

2. Set the stage. Pick his favourite place – whether you consider it
   romantic or not – to pop the question. This might be a secluded camp
   site, a fancy restaurant, a golf course at sunset ... or a bar. Let your
   lover's taste be your guide.

3. Keep your plans flexible. You may have an evening of French cuisine
   and fine wine in mind; he may be in the mood for burgers and beer.
   Unless your plans involve other people or events, go with the flow.

4. Make a splash if your beloved appreciates the theatrical. Put your
   question up in lights at a dance, or bring in a soloist to croon over
   pasta.

5. Keep the occasion subtle if your partner tends to like things more
   subdued. Pop the question over dessert, or during a private game of
   pool.

6. Bring or plan an engagement gift. Of course, you could get him a ring,
   but a puppy with a note tied around its neck might be a better choice.
   Or a motorcycle. Something that will last for a long time.

7. Give him some time to be surprised and tongue-tied. Remember, even
   though he loves you for the unconventional woman you are, he
   probably won't see this one coming.

Warning

If you've already been dropping hints and he hasn't been receptive, don't
use a proposal to force the issue. Your attempt at romance may backfire.

112

Propose Marriage to a Woman

This is a moment that will be recounted over and over to friends, family and even your children. Make it memorable.

⊙ Steps

1   Try to keep your plans to yourself.

2   Consult your intended's father before asking, if you are a traditional kind of guy.

3   Make sure the proposal reflects your personal style. Get on one knee and propose at the top of a mountain, during a romantic weekend or while you're on a tropical holiday.

4   Have champagne and flowers waiting.

5   If your partner says yes, call the people that matter to let them know.

6   Be prepared to start talking about wedding plans immediately.

7   Don't be offended if your new fiancée is not taken with the ring you selected. She can choose another setting later if she desires.

✳ Tip

It may be best to pop the question first and buy the ring together later, especially if you're not sure of her taste.

113

Buy an Engagement Ring

Bucking tradition might be necessary when it comes to selecting an engagement ring that she'll wear for the rest of her life. It's always best to get input from the bride-to-be.

1 Discuss styles, stones and budget with your bride-to-be if you're going to be shopping together.

2 Expect to pay about £2,500 to £3,500 per half carat for a quality diamond. This is a rough estimate that will depend on several factors, including the diamond's size – larger diamonds are rarer, and therefore more valuable (see 151 "Buy a Diamond").

3 Go shopping with your intended after your proposal, or shop alone so that you can surprise her.

4 If you shop alone and aren't sure what style she wants, buy just the stone, make an appointment with a jeweller to return later for a setting, and pop the question using a fun imitation ring. After she's accepted, go back and pick out a setting together.

5 Have the ring made or buy one ready-made, once you've discussed styles with your sweetheart.

Despite the old adage that the ring should be worth two months' salary, if you can't spend that much money, go for a simple design that can be dressed up with the wedding band.

Use the stone from a family heirloom to make a unique and less expensive ring she'll treasure.

If you buy the ring without the bride's input, don't fret if she doesn't like your choice. Get a basic setting with an understanding from the jeweller that you can come back and trade up.

114

Decide on a Form of Wedding Ceremony

Have you always had your heart set on a church wedding? Or does a quiet registry office ceremony sound ideal? Perhaps you like the idea of a civil wedding but fancy an unusual location or one that is special to you. The choice is yours.

1. If you want a church wedding, make an appointment to see the vicar or priest of your local church to discuss the ceremony.

2. If you want to get married in a register office, make an appointment to attend the register office in the district where you live. You can discuss with them the personalisation of your ceremony with special readings and/or music, available dates and the fees involved.

3. Consider getting married at one of more than 3,000 approved premises in England and Wales. These include stately homes and museums, boats, castles and more unusual venues, such as the British Airways London Eye in London and Epsom Racecourse.

4. Once you have chosen your venue, contact the register office in the same district and ask about the availability of the registrar to come out to the venue and the fee involved.

5. Decide whether you would like to get married outside or in your own home. At the moment, the only possibility within the UK is Scotland, where you can marry half-way up a mountain if you choose. Alternatively, you could marry in a register office and arrange your own private ceremony in your garden or an outdoor space special to you to follow immediately afterwards.

6. Consider getting married on a beach in the Seychelles or on a Carribbean island. There are several tour operatours that offer wedding packages in holiday destinations all over the world. Look at a few of them and decide if this is the right option for you.

✳ **Tips**

Look into all the options thoroughly with your intended. You may discover that you have very different ideas about the style of wedding you prefer!

Consider the various costs involved before making the final decision.

Log onto confetti.co.uk for a list of current approved venues for marriage in the UK and abroad.

Plan a Wedding

Now that you've recovered from the delightful shock of your engagement, take a deep breath, grab a notebook and your address book, and then let the countdown to the big day begin!

Steps

1. Imagine your wedding from beginning to end. Where and when have you dreamed the wedding would take place? How formal would you like the event to be? What will the wedding party wear? What kind of food would you like to serve?

2. Pick a date.

3. Set a budget – one that is functional and provides for some flexibility. Here is where you must combine fantasy with practicality.

4. Ask friends and family to recommend a reputable jeweller. Order your engagement and/or wedding rings.

5. Book the wedding and reception sites.

6. Meet with the officiant of your wedding. Now is the time to be clear about rules and restrictions regarding the ceremony and ceremony site.

7. Select your wedding attendants – your wedding party can be as big or small as you like.

8. Choose a dress and wedding attire for the rest of the wedding party.

9. Make a guest list. You may have to compromise on the number of guests if your budget is limited.

10. Plan your pre-wedding parties, ceremony, reception and honeymoon. Consider menus, decorations, favours and music.

11. Interview and hire suppliers: wedding coordinator, photographer, video recordist, caterer, florist and entertainment.

12 Check the legalities relating to obtaining a marriage licence, and how long it will take.

13 Take care of the rest of the paperwork, from ordering invitations to setting up a wedding list.

✸ Tips

Ask your parents early on in the planning stage for their input.

Be kind to yourself and your betrothed—this can be an extremely stressful time.

Keep a notebook to fill with things like swatches of fabric, notes and supplier contracts.

Be sure to take time away with your partner and give attention to your relationship.

116
Create a Successful Marriage

As with most good things, a long and satisfying marriage takes time and effort – on the part of both spouses. Your reward is happiness of the highest order.

◉ Steps

1 Cherish compatibility. Seek out the things that interest, please and delight both of you.

2 Respect and treasure your differences. Learn from one another. Appreciate and understand your spouse's distinctive style, approach and personality – especially when it diverges from yours. Differences can often turn into delight.

3 Cultivate patience. Give your spouse enough time to reach a comfortable middle ground in his or her own way.

4 Learn how to be understanding, and develop the ability to see through your spouse's eyes.

Relationships

5   Share your feelings in regular talk sessions. A nice atmosphere in a good restaurant helps open the doors to intimacy and sharing. Really listen to your partner. Be sure to look directly into the eyes of your loved one.

6   Strive for a high ratio of positive to negative in comments and actions.

7   Allow time to pass when you're surprised by a disappointment. Solutions will become evident when there is patience. A good night's sleep will help additional insights to surface.

8   Resolve the inevitable differences in a way that strengthens and deepens your love. Strive to communicate your feelings without being aggressive or defensive. Listen to each other with an open mind and seek resolutions that you both can be happy with.

9   Learn to express thankfulness for the smallest things. This gratitude can be brief and must be genuine.

❊ **Tip**

Especially after children arrive, schedule time to be alone together, and make it fun. Enjoy each other's company and laugh together.

117

Impress Your In-Laws

In-law jokes have been part of world cultures for centuries. It can sometimes be tricky to forge a positive relationship with your spouse's parents, but it's a good idea to try.

 Steps

1   Treat your spouse well. Nothing pleases parents more than knowing that their son or daughter is being well-loved and cared for.

2   Present a united front. Never squabble with your spouse in front of his or her parents. If you think hot issues may come up, discuss how you will deal with them ahead of time.

3 Contact them without waiting for them to contact you, and invite them to visit before they invite themselves. This allows you to get your home ready and to prepare yourself emotionally for a visit on your own terms.

4 Ask their advice, regardless of whether or not you plan to take it. Your spouse's parents will be glad to feel that they still have some influence in their child's life.

5 Be creative. If it bothers you that your mother-in-law always tries to wash up after dinner at your house, offer her another task, such as serving coffee or playing with the baby.

6 If you and your in-laws are completely incompatible, just handle it as gracefully as possible, avoid contact whenever you can, and remember that even if you will never love your in-laws, they did something wonderful when they created your spouse.

 Tip

Begin making your own cherished family Christmas and New Year traditions at home, especially if the festive period becomes a tug-of-war about whose family to visit and it isn't possible to visit both. Or go away and enjoy the holidays in an entirely different way.

⚠ **Warnings**

Avoid confrontations with your in-laws. Try to let criticism or differences of opinion wash over you.

Try to get along well with your in-laws, but don't let them take over. This can be especially important when children arrive. Set reasonable ground rules for everyone in the family.

Name a Baby

Whether you decide to go with a traditional name or with a more unusual one, make sure the name will fit your baby throughout life.

Steps

1. Decide whether you lean towards unusual names or more traditional ones.

2. Collect names from both partners' family trees. Look for names of people who have played a meaningful role in either of your lives or who have names you both like.

3. Write down your favourite artists and writers; favourite characters from novels, films or plays; and figures from history or mythology.

4. Think about cities and countries significant to you and your partner – geographically inspired names have become popular in recent years.

5. Think about your heritage. Do you want to recognise a particular nationality or ethnic background in your baby's name? Could you use other elements in your family's history, such as place names?

6. Buy a book of baby names and highlight the ones you both like.

7. When you've compiled a list, think about how your favourites sound with the baby's last name. You'll probably want to avoid rhymes, long first names combined with long last names, or combinations that add up to a celebrity's name or a pun, or that have any unflattering nicknames.

8. Using all of the above information, narrow your list down to two girls' names and/or two boys' names (depending on whether you know the sex of the baby).

9. After the baby is born, either bestow a name immediately or, if you prefer, observe your baby for a day or two and decide which of your choices seems most appropriate.

Tip

Try not to divulge your top choice. It's a fun surprise when the day finally comes. Plus, you don't want someone else who's also expecting to poach your favourite name.

Be a Good Parent

A big part of good parenting is establishing respect between parents and children. Your child needs to know what you expect of her, and you in turn must learn to listen and wait.

⊚ Steps

1   Slow down. Babies and children live in a different time frame from adults – usually a much slower one. Keep this in mind as you talk to your child, care for her and go about your day together.

2   Observe your child. You'll be amazed at how well you'll get to know your child by sitting back and watching. This focused awareness will help you better understand moods, abilities and temperament. Listening is important, too.

3   Stay optimistic. Optimism is contagious; so is negativity. Show your child through your behaviour how to overcome minor setbacks. Children emulate their parents' attitudes and habits, so it will help if you have a positive outlook.

4   Accept and acknowledge your child's feelings and desires. Let her know it's OK to feel sad, scared or angry. You can say, "It looks as if you're sad because your friend has gone home" or "It seems that you're cross because I put the ball away".

5   Tell your child your expectations. Children won't always comply right away, but they need to understand clearly what a parent expects: "I want you to put on your sweater. We're going outside", or "I want your feet to stay off the couch".

6   Set appropriate limits. Even when you acknowledge a feeling or desire, you must make a child aware of appropriate behaviour and rules: "I can see you're angry at your friend because he took the toy from you, but I won't let you hit him. Hitting is not something we do in our family. What else can you do?"

7   Wait. Let your child do as much as she can on her own – learn to walk, put on socks, resolve conflicts with friends. Anxiety or the desire to help often tempts parents to rush in and solve the problem for the

child. A better response is to wait and see what your child can manage on her own. She might surprise you.

8　Behave genuinely. Just as you accept your child's moods, though not always her behaviour, it's OK to have a sad or angry thought yourself and express it appropriately: "I'm really tired right now but I'm listening to you". A parent's genuineness prepares a child for life.

9　Look after yourself and your marriage. Make arrangements to have some guilt-free time to take care of your own needs. Plan a date with your partner and forget the kids for a while. You'll be a happier person and a better parent.

❄ Tips

Build more time into your day so you can slow down with your child and enjoy your time together. Continuous hurried behaviour creates stress for both you and your child.

Start a babysitting group with local parents so you can have a few hours to yourself or a night out with your partner. Ask friends, grandparents or a responsible teenager to babysit. Get out of the house and have some adult fun.

⚠ Warning

Monitor your child if he or she is having a dispute with a friend. Feelings can quickly escalate, and a parent may need to intervene. Safety should always be your number one consideration.

120

Get your Child into the Right School

A child's school days are critical to their development, both academically and socially. So choosing the right school may be one of the most important decisions you ever make.

◎ Steps

1　Start thinking seriously about your child's schooling when he or she reaches the age of three. You have to register which school you want your child to attend during the year prior to attendance, so leave yourself plenty of time to weigh up the possibilities.

2 Get a list of local state schools from your Local Education Authority (LEA) or library. Begin by looking at those in your immediate geographic vicinity. Consider the distance and routes between the school and home.

3 Make a shortlist of suitable candidates and call each one, asking for brochures or literature. The manner in which a school deals with such a simple request may give you a clue as to its desirability.

4 Visit the OFSTED web page (ofsted.gov.uk) and check out the government's official report on each of your possible schools.

5 Arrange to visit the school and talk to the headteacher, or other senior member of staff. Always visit during term time: this will give you a more accurate picture of day-to-day life in the school. Pay attention to the general "vibe" of the surroundings: an overly noisy atmosphere and hostile children – not to mention harassed staff – may be warning signs.

6 It's a good idea to apply to more than one school – each one will give you details of its application process.

❋ Tips

Sometimes the school you choose for your child will be over-subscribed. Local Education Authorities usually give precedence to those applicants with siblings already attending the school, or those who live in close proximity. If your child is refused entry because of over-subscription you have the right of appeal to your LEA.

When visiting, always look for signs of success within the confines of the National Curriculum.

Write an Invitation

Your invitation sets the tone for your party – take time to think about what you want it to communicate.

Steps

1   Decide on the tone, voice and level of formality you're going to use, based on the event itself. This will dictate whether you handwrite the cards or have them printed, and whether you choose a pre-printed or personalised invitation.

2   Consider making a theme invitation – using such items as travel postcards, photographs and envelopes studded with confetti – for a casual, festive occasion.

3   Choose the type of card you want, and order or buy a few more than you think you'll need. This will permit you to add some guests to your list at the last minute, if necessary.

4   Determine the wording based on the level of formality. For example, a formal invitation might say, "Dr and Mrs Stanley request the pleasure of your company," whereas a more casual note might say, "Please join us."

5   Include the names of the host and/or hostess, as well as the place, time, date and purpose of the party, even if it's a simple get-together. Make sure to add RSVP information.

6   Include a respond-by date in a formal invitation so you can get an accurate head count in time to adjust the amount of food, number of place settings and room size. For a wedding, charity function or other formal event, consider including a response card and a stamped, self-addressed envelope inside the big envelope.

7   Post invitations three weeks before most events, four weeks before a formal affair. For events held during the Christmas season send invitations around the end of November.

Use precisely the kind of RSVP method that best serves the occasion: a response card for a head count, a telephone number for expediency, or an e-mail address if you know that the invitees have computers.

Large dinner parties, receptions and weddings call for written invitations.

Count out those who don't reply, but be prepared for a few who haven't replied to show up.

Printing invitations costs much more but is worthwhile if you are planning a formal or large event.

122

Reply to a Written Invitation

Replying to an invitation properly demonstrates your good manners, and it is also a mark of respect and consideration for your host.

◎ Steps

1 Read the invitation carefully. Often it gives a hint as to a preferred mode of reply.

2 If a response card with envelope is provided, fill it out and send it off in a timely manner. If the invitation gives a phone number, call as soon as you know whether you will attend.

3 Use your personal headed stationery or a blank card to respond to a formal invitation that doesn't come with a response card. Write some variation of the following: "Joseph Mackenzie and guest, Rachel Helfond, accept with pleasure the invitation to dine with the Bletchley-Smythes on 28 October 2003."

4 If you cannot attend, send your regrets: "I regret that I will not be attending the dinner party, as I will be away."

5 Post the reply in time to assure that you are giving your host at least one week's notice.

RSVP is an abbreviation for the French phrase *répondez s'il vous plaît,* which means "please reply".

⚠ Warning

If you don't reply – unless specifically instructed not to – your host's horrified face shouldn't surprise you when you make an appearance anyway.

123

Buy a Wedding Present

Wish the lucky pair well with a heartfelt and useful gift.

◉ Steps

1   If the couple has a wedding list registered at a department store, the details may be enclosed with your wedding invitation. If they're not, phone a member of the wedding party to find out.

2   Search the wedding list, making sure you have the full names of both bride and groom, as well as the wedding date, to make the search easier. The list should provide an updated list of gifts the couple hasn't yet received.

3   Select a gift from the list that's within your price range, even if that means you can only buy one cup and saucer.

4   Ask for the present to be gift-wrapped.

5   Address the gifts to the bride before the wedding, and to both the bride and groom afterwards.

6   Arrange to have your gift sent in advance of the wedding instead of bringing it to the wedding; this is much easier for the wedding party. Most department stores will post your gift for you, especially if you order it online or by telephone.

7   If you prefer to give money instead of a gift, present it on the day of
    the ceremony. Make a cheque payable to both the bride and groom.

✳ Tips

As a rule of thumb, select a gift from the list since the couple has
expressly requested these items. Refrain from buying a print by your
favourite artist or an antique cake platter you love unless you are
absolutely positive the couple will also love it.

Consider purchasing a large gift with a group of friends.

Shop early when buying a gift from the list. You'll have a wider choice in
your price range.

⚠ Warning

Avoid monogramming your gift. The couple can't return or exchange a
monogrammed gift, and you may not know what names the couple will
choose.

124

Be a Proper Wedding Guest

**Bear in mind these quick pointers for being a perfect wedding
guest, and you'll help the wedding day go smoothly for the
bride and groom.**

◉ Steps

1   Make your hotel and travel reservations early, especially if you receive
    a "save the date" notice.

2   Purchase your wedding present early, and use the list. It is designed
    to make your life – and the lives of the bride and groom – easier.

3   Reply as soon as possible after you get the invitation. Bring a guest
    only if you receive an invitation addressed to you and a guest.

4   Dress appropriately. If the invitation says black tie, men should wear
    dinner jackets and women should wear formal dresses. If you are

unsure of the dress code, you're safer erring on the side of dressing up too much.

5   Bring children only if the invitation expressly mentions them. Weddings are formal events and typically not appropriate for little ones.

6   Arrive 15 minutes before the ceremony begins. Tradition dictates that friends and family of the bride sit on the left and friends and family of the groom sit on the right. Typically, an usher will lead you to your seat.

7   Wait in the receiving line, if there is one, to congratulate the newlywed couple and their parents after the ceremony. Keep your greeting upbeat and brief.

8   Remain quiet and attentive during toasts at the reception, and while the couple cuts the wedding cake.

9   Wait for the bride and groom to have their first dance before you hit the dance floor. Then get up, dance and enjoy the party; the couple will be pleased to see all their guests having a good time.

10   Avoid engaging the bride or groom in conversation for too long – they have many guests to greet, and a honeymoon suite awaits them.

✳ Tips

If you have questions about attire, whether you can bring children to the ceremony, or other logistics, call the best man or maid of honour, who is often much more accessible than the bride or groom.

Bear in mind that the bride and groom want to see and talk to every guest, so don't feel disappointed if you don't get to chat with them for long.

Post your present ahead of time to make it easier for the bride and groom. If instead you bring it with you, take it to the reception and place it on the gift table.

Be a Proper Guest at a Party

A good guest responds promptly to the invitation, arrives fashionably late, is cheerful and friendly, and isn't the last one to go home.

Steps

1　Reply to the invitation in a timely manner. Use the method indicated: phone, post or e-mail.

2　Bring a friend only if you receive an invitation for you and a guest. Your hosts may have a food, budget or space limitation.

3　Go with the spirit of the party. If it's for a special occasion, such as a housewarming, bring a gift. If it's dressy, wear your glad rags. Costume required? Dig into your wardrobe and get creative.

4　Prepare. Read up on current events; think of a few good stories; recall a few films, books or plays. Try hard not to be shy or moody – for your host's sake, if not your own.

5　Arrive reasonably close to the starting time. The starting time for a cocktail party tends to be looser than it is for a dinner party, which requires punctuality. Fashionably late means no more than 30 minutes past the indicated time.

6　Seek out your host or hostess and say hello as soon as you arrive.

7　Make an effort to mix and mingle cheerfully. Don't just hide in a corner chatting with people you already know.

8　Know your alcohol limits and don't exceed them. Take into consideration your energy level, food intake and drink size. Nothing's ruder than ruining a party with inappropriate behaviour.

9　Treat your host's home as you would your own – no wet glasses on the furniture, no cigarettes ground out in the plants, no cocktail sticks on the floor. Don't smoke without asking permission.

10 Leave at a reasonable hour. Some hosts close the bar half an hour before they want the party to end. Take a hint when others start slipping on their coats.

11 Find your hosts to say thank you and goodbye personally. It's also thoughtful to call the next day and let your host know how much you enjoyed the event.

✳ Tips

If you know your hosts, you might call and ask about the dress code, if the invitation doesn't make it clear. Or ask another guest who's attending.

Unless it's clear that this is not necessary, bring something to drink, whether or not it's alcoholic.

⚠ Warning

Never arrive early; your hosts may not be ready to receive guests.

126

Introduce People

Want to meet new people and improve your social graces? Here's how to make proper introductions at parties, dinners and other social situations.

◉ Steps

1 Introduce individuals to each other using both first and last names.

2 If you're introducing someone who has a title – a doctor, for example – include the title as well as the first and last names in the introduction.

3 Introduce the younger or less prominent person to the older or more prominent person, regardless of the sex of the individuals. (However, if a considerable age difference lies between the two, it is far more courteous to make introductions in deference to age, regardless of social rank.) For example: "Arthur Dent, I'd like you to meet Dr Gertrude Smith."

Etiquette

4   If the person you are introducing has a specific relationship to you, make the relationship clear by adding a phrase such as "my boss", "my wife" or "my uncle". In the case of unmarried couples who are living together, "companion" and "partner" are good choices.

5   Use your spouse's first and last name if he or she has a different last name than you. Include the phrase "my wife" or "my husband".

6   Introduce an individual to the group first, then the group to the individual. For example: "Dr Brown, I'd like you to meet my friends Kim Howe, Simon Campbell and Michael Vince. Everyone, this is Dr Kurt Brown."

✳ Tips

If you've forgotten a name, you'll seem impolite if you try to ignore the need for the introduction. It's less awkward (and better manners) to apologise and acknowledge that the name has escaped you.

If your host neglects to introduce you to other guests, feel free to introduce yourself, but make your relationship to the host clear in your introduction.

127

Shake Hands

Historically used to show that both people were unarmed, the handshake today is a critical gauge of confidence, trust, sophistication and mood.

◉ Steps

1   Extend your right hand to meet the other person's right hand.

2   Point your thumb upwards towards the other person's arm and extend your arm at a slight downward angle.

3   Wrap your hand around the other person's hand when your thumb joints come together.

4   Grasp the hand firmly and squeeze gently once. Remember that limp
    handshakes are a big turnoff, as are bone-crushing grasps.

5   Hold the handshake for two to three seconds.

6   Pump your hand up and down a few times to convey sincerity. (This
    gesture is optional.)

✳ Tip

A two-handed handshake is not for first meetings. It is a sign of real
affection, and you should reserve it for friends and intimates.

⚠ Warning

Handshakes are not appropriate in all cultures. Investigate local customs
if you will be visiting a foreign country.

128

Remember Names

The ability to remember the names of people you meet will
always serve you well in social situations.

⊙ Steps

1   Pay attention when you are introduced to someone. A few minutes
    after you meet the person, say his or her name to yourself again. If
    you have forgotten it, talk to the person again and ask for the name.

2   Write down the new name three times while picturing the person's
    face; do this as soon as possible after meeting someone.

3   Ask how to spell a difficult name, or glance at the spelling on the
    person's business card, if it's offered. If you know the spelling of a
    word and can picture it in your mind, you'll remember it better.

4   Connect a name to a common word you will remember. For
    example, the name Salazar could sound like "salamander", "bazaar"
    or "sell a jar".

5   Make a connection to the person's hobby or employment. "Bill the pill" might help you remember the name of a pharmacist, for example.

Tip

Writing down new names is generally a very successful memorising technique that doesn't require a lot of work.

129

Propose a Toast

A few carefully selected words can add a personal touch to any social gathering. People make toasts over festive drinks, such as champagne or sparkling wine.

Steps

1   Let the host or hostess make the first toast at a dinner party. If she or he does not do so, initiate a toast after the plates from the main course are cleared.

2   Make certain that everyone, no matter what he or she is drinking, has a full glass to raise.

3   Stand up and tap your glass to get everyone's attention.

4   For a formal occasion, have everyone (except for the person you are toasting) stand up. If it is less formal, guests may remain seated.

5   Direct your toast towards the host or hostess or the guest of honour. Speak loudly and slowly so that everyone can hear you.

6   Keep it brief, sincere and to the point; choose simple but substantial words to convey your feelings. Some of the best toasts are just a single sentence or two.

7   If you are feeling more creative, you can begin with an appropriate quotation, a poem or an amusing anecdote.

8. Consider mentioning an unusually brave, heroic, romantic or awesome act performed by the person you are honouring.

9. Weave humour into your toast, but don't embarrass the person you are honouring. If the assembled group is close-knit, it's all right to refer to shared experiences, but don't make the toast a private joke between you and a few of the people present.

10. When you have finished your toast, lift your glass to the recipient and lead the group in drinking to that person.

✳ Tips

If you know ahead of time that you will be giving a toast, write down some thoughts on note cards and practise delivering the toast before the big event.

Remember that the toast puts the spotlight on the person being honoured, not on you.

If you are the recipient of a toast, remain seated and refrain from drinking when everyone drinks to you.

⚠ Warning

Make sure your toast is appropriate for everyone at the event. For example, a best man's speech at a wedding ceremony shouldn't refer to stag night escapades.

130

Leave a Party Graciously

Arriving at the party is the easy part. When you are ready to leave, exercise tact and always thank the host or hostess before you depart.

Steps

1. Wait until the host is not in conversation or caught in the middle of cooking or serving duties.

2   Express your gratitude for the invitation, and compliment the host on
    one particular aspect of the party.

3   Make a tentative reference to the next time you will see each other.
    For example, saying "We should get together for drinks soon" takes
    the emphasis off your departure.

4   Acknowledge everyone in the room, if possible. If the party is too large
    to permit this, express a parting gesture to those guests with whom
    you spent time talking.

5   Make your parting words short and sweet in an attempt to let
    everyone else get back to the festivities.

✳ Tips

Avoid long and effusive apologies. Others will look upon your departure
negatively if you insist on apologising for it.

If the party invitation included an ending time, don't stay too long after
the time indicated.

131

Write a Thank-You Note

You can fill even short thank-you notes with appreciation and
meaning. And remember, "better late than never" applies – the
recipient will always enjoy your thanks.

 Steps

1   Mention the gift, favour or party you attended.

2   Talk about the appropriateness of the gift or favour: "Your baby-sitting
    for my children has truly been a lifesaver in these difficult times." (You
    can describe a gift that didn't quite suit your taste as "a conversation
    piece" or "unique").

3   Tie the appropriateness of the gift to the person who gave it to you:
    "You've always understood my taste in clothes."

4   Talk about how you plan to use the gift (or substitute this step for step 2): "I have a picture of my parents that would look perfect in your frame." If you received a gift of money, mention how you will spend it.

5   Add a small personal note to update the giver about your life: "I have completely recovered from my cold and plan to hit the slopes again as soon as I can."

6   Consider sending a token of appreciation along with your note if you're thanking someone for a good deed. Possibilities include flowers, chocolate or an invitation to lunch (your treat).

☀ Tips

Many people consider it unnecessary to write thank-you notes for gifts given in person, with the exception of wedding gifts, as long as you thank the giver verbally. But when in doubt, a written note is always a good idea.

A newly married couple should write individual, handwritten notes to all gift givers, and post these within three months of the wedding (at the very latest).

Send a thank-you note for birthday and holiday gifts within three days of when you receive them.

132

Make a Dry Martini

The classic, elegant martini has undergone quite a resurgence lately. Makes one martini.

◎ Steps

1   Pour gin and vermouth over ice in a cocktail shaker.

2   Shake or stir well.

3   Strain into a chilled martini glass.

4   Serve straight up with an olive. (To make this drink a Gibson, serve with a pickled onion.)

❑ gin

❑ dash of extra-dry vermouth

❑ 3 or 4 ice cubes

❑ cocktail olive

133

Make a Cosmopolitan

A Cosmopolitan is a fruity, refreshing drink of fairly recent origin that has become a classic. Makes one serving.

⊙ Steps

1 Wet the rim of a chilled martini glass with cranberry juice in a saucer and dip in sugar in another saucer.

2 Put ice in a cocktail shaker.

3 Add the vodka, cranberry juice, lime juice and Cointreau to the ice.

4 Shake twice.

5 Strain into the cocktail glass.

6 Add a lemon twist.

Ingredients

❑ 30 ml (1 fl oz) cranberry juice plus extra for dipping glasses

❑ granulated sugar

❑ 3 or 4 ice cubes

❑ 50 ml (2 fl oz) vodka

❑ 30 ml (1 fl oz) lime juice

❑ dash of Cointreau

❑ lemon twist

Mix a Frozen Margarita

Break out the tortilla chips and salsa: you're making frozen margaritas! Just serve them as soon as they're made, for best results. Makes one serving.

Steps

1. Rub a cut lime around the rim of a margarita glass and then dip the glass into a plate of coarse salt if desired.

2. Put the tequila, fresh lime juice and triple sec or Cointreau in a blender with the crushed ice.

3. Blend at medium speed for 5 to 10 seconds and pour immediately.

4. Garnish with a lime wedge.

Ingredients

❏ cut lime

❏ coarse salt

❏ 50 ml (2 fl oz) tequila

❏ 25 ml (¾ fl oz) fresh lime juice

❏ 30 ml (1 fl oz) triple sec or Cointreau

❏ crushed ice

❏ lime wedge

Choose Wine for a Special Occasion

Whether the occasion is a birthday or a christening, a discreet lovers' tryst or a formal dinner party, a quality wine is often what is required. But which wine should you choose?

⊙ Steps

General Points

1 Consider the price that you are prepared to pay. Decent wines can be bought for £5 and upwards, and some quite excellent ones for between £10 and £20. But if you really want to impress, there are wines available at luxury prices in the hundreds of pounds.

2 Decide whether you intend to buy a wine to be drunk on its own or with food. Remember that if you are buying a wine to go with a meal being cooked by someone else, your choice may not match the food.

3 Decide on the general characteristics of the wine that you want to buy. Do you want a white wine that is sweet or one that is dry? Are you looking for a red that is light and fruity or heavy and oaky? Learn to read wine labels carefully, since they will inform you on these characteristics.

4 Remember that you are not buying the wine for your own satisfaction but for another or others. Give primacy to their tastes. If you don't know what their tastes are, ask them. There is no point in buying a good bottle of white wine to share with a person who only ever drinks red.

5 Know that a shot in the dark – buying a wine by the attractions of its label, name or price – will often lead to disappointment. Discuss your choice with an experienced and honest vintner if you possibly can. Alternatively, take advice from friends.

Specifics

1 Choose a sparkling white wine as the universally acknowledged drink for celebrations of all kinds. Buy a sparkling wine that is bone dry and

ensure that it is thoroughly chilled. Select French Champagne if you can afford it – it is still unrivalled in its prestige.

2 Buy a white wine for drinking as an aperitif before food or with nibbles. Select a New Zealand Sauvignon Blanc, rather than a similar wine from France. Choose a Chardonnay from Australia or California, where the extra sunshine brings a flavour rich in fruit.

3 For an intimate evening with love in the air, try a sweet desert wine such as a Muscat or Beaumes de Venise. Consume with some light and tasty sweet food, such as Italian cantucci or a good quality ice cream.

4 Choose a hefty vintage red wine to impress as your contribution to a dinner party. Ensure that, if you hand the bottle over to your host on arrival, he or she is aware that the wine requires to be uncorked immediately – it will need to "breathe" before it is consumed.

✳ Tips

Educate yourself about wines before you confront this situation. Read about the different regions and grape varieties – there is information available in books, magazines and on the Internet. Above all, experiment with a range of wines and build up a personal taste.

If possible buy a wine that you already know and like, even if it's not especially fancy. One advantage is that you aren't likely to be disappointed. Also, you'll be able to proffer the wine with a personal recommendation, which usually creates a good impression.

136

Open a Wine Bottle

It's actually pretty simple to open a bottle of wine. These steps are for a double-action, or wing, corkscrew, which has two arms (or wings) that help lever the cork out of the bottle.

◎ Steps

1 Remove the top of the foil by cutting around the rim of the bottle with the sharp point of the corkscrew. The arms of the corkscrew will have

to be raised for this step. You can also make a slit in the foil and remove the whole thing before beginning.

2 Stand the bottle on a flat, hard surface at mid-chest level or lower. Lower the arms of the corkscrew. Holding the corkscrew as vertically and straight as possible, place the sharp end directly into the middle of the cork.

3 Securely grasp the top of the bottle and the lower end of the corkscrew with one hand.

4 With the other hand, begin turning the handle of the corkscrew clockwise, applying an even, constant downward pressure into the cork. As the corkscrew goes into the cork, its arms will begin to rise.

5 Apply more pressure if the corkscrew will not penetrate the cork.

6 Keep turning the handle until the arms of the corkscrew are completely raised and the screw is well into the cork.

7 With one hand on each arm of the corkscrew, press the arms down. This will lift the cork out of the bottle.

8 Wrap your hand around the base of the corkscrew and lift straight up.

9 Remove the foil, if necessary.

10 Twist the cork off the corkscrew.

11 Wipe the rim of the bottle with a clean, damp towel before serving, to remove any stray pieces of cork.

✳ Tips

Avoid corkscrews that penetrate the cork with a solid, ridged metal screw, which won't grip a cork well and can tear it apart. Instead, use a corkscrew with a metal spiral resembling a cartoon pig's tail.

If for some reason you just can't get the cork out on the first try, twist the corkscrew into a different part of the cork until the arms are raised, and repeat the process. But if you keep turning the corkscrew handle until the arms are completely raised, you shouldn't need to do this.

Things You'll Need

❑ double-action (wing) corkscrew

Style and Etiquette

Choosing the right wine for a meal can strike fear into the heart of a host. There are no hard-and-fast rules – you're best advised to serve the wine that you personally feel will complement the dish. If you're still unsure, check below for some guidelines.

Seafood

- Pair a delicate-flavoured fish such as sole or plaice with delicate wines: a Muscadet or Vouvray from France, or a Sauvignon Blanc from New Zealand.

- For fuller-flavoured fish such as trout or sea bass, consider a full-bodied Chardonnay or one of the lighter red wines.

- For rich seafood such as salmon, consider a Chablis, a full-bodied Chardonnay or an elegant pinot noir.

- For shellfish such as oysters, crisp Muscadet, Chablis and sparkling wine are classic. For richer shellfish, such as lobster, try a Chardonnay or a Chablis.

- For spicy seafood dishes, try a spicy wine such as a Gewürztraminer from Alsace, a New Zealand Riesling, or alternatively a dry sparkling wine.

Meat

- For grilled meats, choose intense, smoky reds: Italian Barolo or Barbaresco, a big Napa Valley Cabernet Sauvignon or an Australian Shiraz.

- Pair full-flavoured dishes such as pepper steak with spicy reds such as Grenache from California, Australia or Gigondas in France. Also good: Côtes-du-Rhône or a peppery Californian Zinfandel.

- For hearty, spicy stews, pick spicy Syrah-based Rhône wines from Hermitage and Côte-Rôtie or California's Central Coast. Zinfandel is another option.

- Lighter meats can sometimes go well with big or off-dry whites. Try an oaky Chardonnay with veal, for example, or a Riesling or Gewürztraminer with baked ham.

reference

Poultry

- Pair delicately flavoured chicken dishes with crisp, delicate white wines such as Vouvray, Muscadet or Sauvignon Blanc.

- For any grilled poultry, try a medium-bodied red Burgundy or Pinot Noir, a South American Cabernet or a fruity Californian Zinfandel.

- For heavily spiced chicken or turkey, try a spicy white wine, such as a Gewürztraminer from Alsace.

- For rich duck dishes, consider a rich, gamey red from Burgundy, Hermitage or Châteauneuf-du-Pape, or a wine high on acidity such as Italian Sangiovese or a white Burgundy.

- Pair game birds with earthy reds: a Rioja or Châteauneuf-du-Pape – or even a mature Cabernet-based wine.

Vegetarian

- Pair strongly flavoured dishes, such as those made with garlic, with robust reds: Syrah or Cabernet Sauvignon. Try a Sangiovese for tomato-based dishes.

- For more subtle dishes, try a crisp white: a Sauvignon Blanc from New Zealand or a Vouvray from France.

- For strong, mushroomy dishes, select Pinot Noir for its delicate, earthy aromas.

- For Mexican dishes with sweetcorn or green chillies, try a crisp Chablis or a slightly grassy New Zealand Sauvignon Blanc – as long as the dish isn't too spicy.

- For spicy dishes, such as curry, try a slightly sweet German Riesling, a Gewürztraminer or a French rosé.

Choose Champagne

Sparkling wine – called Champagne if it comes from the Champagne region of France – is made from Chardonnay, Pinot Noir, Muscat and other grape varieties.

Steps

1   Learn to look for the words "méthode champenoise" on the label. True Champagnes and the best sparkling wines from other regions are made by this process of double-fermentation – once in barrels or vats and a second time in bottles.

2   Learn the different types of sparkling wines, from extra-brut (the driest) to extra-sec (very dry), sec (dry), demi-sec and doux (sweet). The great vintage Champagnes are found in the brut category.

3   Taste various types of sparkling wine and Champagne to get an idea of what kinds appeal most to you. One way to do this is to check the wine seller's events calendars and attend Champagne tastings.

4   Ask friends whose taste you respect for advice and recommendations, and talk to wine sellers, too.

5   Learn the histories and winemaking styles of various sparkling wine houses in France, California and elsewhere. Remember that Germany, Spain and Italy also make sparkling wines.

Tips

Sparkling wine terms can be confusing. "Brut," for example, is drier than "extra dry."

Only sparkling wines from the Champagne region of France are correctly called Champagnes – but the term is still casually used for all sparkling wines, especially in the United States. Some California sparkling wines will even say "Champagne" on the label.

Less expensive sparkling wines are usually made by the charmat bulk process, in which all the fermentation takes place in vats.

139

Open a Champagne Bottle

It takes some skill to open a bottle of Champagne so that the bubbly ends up in the flutes and not all over your guests.

◎Steps

1 Remove the foil from the cork.

2 Angle the bottle away from everyone so that if the cork pops out, it won't injure anyone.

3 Untwist the wire restraint securing the cork.

4 Wrap the bottle's neck and cork in a clean napkin.

5 Take hold of the cork with the napkin and gently untwist.

6 Continue untwisting, or hold the cork in place and twist the bottle itself.

7 Slowly ease the cork out of the bottle's neck. Wait for a soft pop. Pour.

✳Tips

Keep glasses nearby and ready to catch the foam.

To preserve and best appreciate the effervescence of any sparkling wine, use the tall, narrow glasses known as flutes. Old-fashioned wide Champagne glasses allegedly cause bubbles to dissipate quickly.

140

Make Mulled Wine

This comforting hot drink is easy to prepare and is a great warmer on a cold winter's night or for a festive pre-Christmas drink, especially if served with warm mince pies.

◎Steps

1 Pour the wine into a large saucepan and add the spices and sugar.

2   Lightly pound the orange and lemon zest to release the aromatic oils, and place it in the wine.

3   Heat slowly so that all the flavours infuse, but do not allow it to boil.

4   Pour the wine into a bowl and ladle it out, hot, into glasses.

5   Add a lemon or orange slice to each glass to decorate.

6   Lace with brandy if desired.

Ingredients

- ❏ 1 l (1³/₄ pt) red wine (usually claret or burgundy)
- ❏ 2 tbsp soft brown sugar
- ❏ 6 cloves
- ❏ 1 cinnamon stick
- ❏ nutmeg
- ❏ zest of 1 orange and 1 lemon
- ❏ orange or lemon slices
- ❏ brandy (optional)

141

Make Egg Nog

"Nog" derives from an old English term for strong ale or liquor. However, this version can be made plain or spiked. Makes eight small servings.

Steps

1   Heat the milk, cloves and peppercorns over low heat in a non-reactive saucepan until the mixture steams and is very hot.

2   Meanwhile, place the egg yolks, nutmeg, sugar and vanilla in a bowl and beat thoroughly.

3   When the milk mixture is hot, turn off the heat and strain out the cloves and peppercorns.

4   Start whisking the egg yolk mixture vigorously, and slowly ladle about 4 tablespoons of milk into it.

5   Switch the whisk to the saucepan and whisk the hot milk while slowly pouring the egg/milk mixture into the saucepan.

6   Return the saucepan to a low heat and stir continuously with a wooden spoon or heatproof flexible spatula. Make sure to stir the mixture off the bottom so the portion in contact with the pan doesn't overcook. The mixture will thicken as it cooks.

7   Test to see if it is ready by dipping the spoon or spatula in the mixture and dragging your finger across the back of it; the eggnog is done when your finger leaves a path through the thickened milk and the milk doesn't run. (This might take as long as 20 minutes. Keep the heat low and don't rush it, or you might curdle the eggs.)

8   Pour the mixture into a mixing bowl. Stir in the remaining extracts and, if you wish, single cream to taste.

9   Chill thoroughly before serving.

❄ Tips

If rum essence is not available, substitute ½ tsp orange essence.

To spike this egg nog recipe, add a dash of rum, brandy or whisky per serving.

Ingredients

☐ 600 ml (1 pt) whole milk

☐ 5 or 6 cloves

☐ 10 white peppercorns

☐ 6 egg yolks

☐ ½ tsp nutmeg

☐ 175 g (6 oz) sugar

☐ 1 tsp. vanilla essence

☐ 1 tsp rum essence

☐ ½ tsp almond essence

☐ single cream (optional)

Set the Table

Whether your dinner is very formal or not so formal, there are a few basic guidelines to setting a table.

Steps

1   Consider how many guests will be attending. If several children will be in attendance, consider having a children's table. If you would like to include the children at the main table, consider booster seats if the children are small.

2   Determine where everyone should sit. For convenience, the cook may want to sit near the kitchen door. Parents should sit next to their children. If there is a male guest, he is traditionally seated on the hostess's right. A female guest is traditionally seated on the host's right. For large parties, determine who would interact best with each other. Some hosts like to alternate men and women, but this isn't necessary. You may want to use place cards to avoid everyone rushing for a seat at the last minute.

3   Decide if you will use a tablecloth. If the tablecloth is damask, you will need a pad under it to prevent it slipping. Also, the middle crease should be arranged so that it runs in a straight and unwavering line down the centre of the table from head to foot. The tablecloth should hang down about 45 cm (18 in) for a seated dinner. For a buffet table, it should hang down to the floor.

4   Once you've put the tablecloth, if you're using one, on the table, you can set it. Begin by folding napkins and placing them in the centre of each diner's place.

5   Place the large dinner fork to the left of the napkin and the smaller dinner fork to the left of the larger fork.

6   Place a side plate to the left of the forks. The dinner plate should not be on the table when guests sit down.

7   Place a knife to the right of the napkin. For poultry or meat, you might want to use steak knives.

8 Place a small knife to the right of the large knife. This knife is used to butter bread, which is placed on the side plate.

9 If serving soup, place a soup spoon to the right of the knives.

10 For dessert, either place a small dessert spoon (and/or fork) horizontally across the top of the setting, or place a dessert spoon to the left of the large dinner knife, and a dessert fork to the right of the large dinner fork. (You can also wait and bring the dessert spoons or forks out just before dessert.)

11 Place a water glass about 5 cm (2 in) above the knife. Place wine glasses to the right of the water glass and slightly closer to the dinner guest.

12 If you will be serving coffee, the cup and saucer should go to the right of the glasses; or bring out the coffee cups when serving the coffee.

Things You'll Need

❏ tablecloth

❏ napkins

❏ silverware

❏ china

❏ glasses for water

❏ wine glasses

❏ coffee cups and saucers

143

Eat at a Formal Dinner

The cutlery is placed on the table in the order in which it will be used, starting with the outside pieces. Let this be your guide as you work your way through a meal.

⊙ Steps

1 Put your napkin on your lap. Unfold it, but don't spread it.

2 If you are offered bread, place it on the side plate to the left of the forks. Use the small knife to butter the bread

3 Use the outside fork for the first course, unless soup is served – then use the soup spoon to the right of the knife.

4 When you are finished with the course, place your fork at the right end of your plate, on a slight diagonal. This signifies that you have finished. For a soup course or another course that uses a wide bowl, place the spoon on the plate below the bowl. If a shallow bowl is used, place the spoon on the bowl in the same manner as a fork on a plate.

5 Use the largest knife and fork to eat your main course.

6 For dessert, use the dessert spoon and/or fork, which are either at your plate's head or closest to your plate on either side.

7 Drink water from the largest glass at your setting.

8 Drink red wine from the rounder glass; drink white wine from the narrower glass.

9 If a little bowl of water is on the table at your place, or appears with the dessert, it is a fingerbowl. Wash the tips of your fingers in it. Dry them with your napkin.

10 Place your napkin on your chair if you leave the table temporarily. Place it next to your plate (don't fold it) when you leave the table.

 Tips

It is proper etiquette for the guests to wait for the host or hostess to unfold the napkin and begin eating before they do the same.

If you're uncertain about how or when to use a certain utensil, watch others and do what the majority of them do.

When eating bread, tear off pieces with your fingers – don't cut it or take bites from larger pieces. Also, butter the piece you've just torn just before you eat it; don't butter the whole piece first.

To eat soup, dip the spoon into the soup, then remove it in a motion away from your body, not towards it. Quietly sip the soup off the side of the spoon, rather than placing the whole spoon in your mouth.

Tie a Tie

Once you've mastered the technique, you won't need a mirror to look dapper in your favourite tie. These instructions will teach you how to tie a four-in-hand knot.

⊚ Steps

1 Lift up the collar of your shirt and put the tie around the back of your neck. The wide end should hang down about twice as low as the thin end; it can hang closer to your right or left hand, depending on what's most comfortable for you.

2 Wrap the wide end around the thin end twice, a few inches below your neck. The wide end should go over the thin end at first.

3 After wrapping the wide end around the second time, push it up through the gap between your chin and the partially formed knot.

4 Tuck the wide end through the front loop of the knot.

5 Gently pull down on both the thin and wide ends below the knot until it is tight.

6 Hold the thin end and slide the knot up to your neck.

7 If the thin end hangs below the wide end, untie the tie and begin again, with the wide end hanging lower than it did the first time.

8 If the wide end hangs too low, untie the tie and begin again, with the wide end hanging higher than it did the first time.

9 Flip your collar back down once you and your tie look dapper.

✳ Tip

When untying a tie, follow the directions in reverse rather than just pulling the narrow end through the knot. Otherwise, you may distort the shape of the tie.

✓ 145 Dress to Flatter Your Figure

Not all of us are able – or willing – to spend hours in the gym in quest of a perfect body, so it's good to know that there are much less painful ways to hide flaws and enhance attributes. Here's how to meet a few common fashion challenges.

Minimise a large bottom

- Wear wide-leg trousers. Steer clear of back pockets or any detailing around the buttocks. Opt for styles that hang full from the middle of the bottom. Front pleats and pockets will help balance your silhouette.
- Choose full or A-line skirts that hang loosely.
- Pair a short jacket with a long skirt and a long jacket with a shorter skirt.
- Select jackets that are slightly fitted and taper gently.
- Wear "empire" dresses for evening. Avoid clingy bias-cut styles.
- Attract admirers' eyes to your upper body. Wear brightly coloured or patterned tops and consider neckline accessories.
- Wear slimming dark colours such as navy, dark brown, charcoal and black.

Make breasts appear larger

- Stand up straight.
- Buy a padded push-up bra.
- Insert foam pads into your bra. Place them in special pockets built into the bra, or place them in the cup under the breast.
- Apply blusher, a shade darker than your skin tone, between the breasts to suggest shadows and cleavage.
- Remember that too much padding or blusher can be obvious. Try to go for a subtle, subliminal effect.
- Wear a tight Lycra top over your bra and under your shirt to add an extra layer.
- Choose clothing material that hugs and draws attention to the bustline.

Minimise a large stomach

- Direct attention towards your upper body. Accessorise your neckline or choose tops with detailing above the breasts.

- Choose trousers with a narrow or tapered leg. Leggings and ski pants are great if they are not too tight.

- Select skirts that do not gather at the waist. Straight skirts will narrow your silhouette.

- Wear tunic-style tops and jumpers, and square jackets that cover the stomach.

- Look for sheath dresses that create a column from your shoulders to your lower leg.

- Avoid belted or drawstring looks, which draw attention to your waist.

- Choose trousers with details around the turn-ups to draw attention down your leg and away from your stomach.

Appear more slender

- Choose clothing all in one colour to give yourself a long, lean look.

- Wear black, which looks slimming.

- Avoid shapeless clothing. Loose clothes often make you appear wider or heavier.

- Choose softly tailored – not tight – pieces, which define but don't constrain.

- Steer clear of horizontal stripes, which make you appear wider.

- Consider vertical stripes, which make you look longer and leaner.

- Wear blocks of colour that draw the eye away from less-than-perfect areas.

- Wear shoulder pads and wide necklines.

- Choose trousers with narrow or tapered legs.

Buy a Perfect Little Black Dress

Every woman needs a little black dress. It's the one garment you can always slip on when you aren't sure what to wear for the evening, but you need to look fabulous.

Steps

1. Think about your body type. If you need to wear a bra when you go out for the evening, you may not be comfortable in halter-neck tops, backless numbers and sheer shoulders. But remember that there are plenty of other ways to look sexy.

2. Identify your key assets. Is your back worth showing off? Want to expose a little shoulder? Is the low-cut look for you? Do your legs deserve the spotlight?

3. Find a dress that's comfortable. Eliminate any dress that makes it hard to walk, sit or dance.

4. Choose a well-constructed dress of a good fabric – a light wool or silk crepe is best – with a lining. The lining will smooth your figure so the shell hangs neatly.

5. Follow the 3:1 ratio – three parts conservative to one part racy. Choose a little black dress that's plain except for that one saucy feature: crisscross straps in back; a daring neckline; a deep slit in the side, back or front.

6. Accessorise for understated drama: fishnet stockings, a bold bracelet, a choker, or leopardskin shoes with a matching bag.

Tip

Surprisingly, some well-made spaghetti-strap dresses work well even if you're on the busty side – they offer a good way to show a little skin without feeling too exposed.

Dress for a Cocktail Party – Men

Cocktail parties give you a chance to mingle among friends, acquaintances, and current and potential business associates. Look sharp and dress appropriately for the occasion.

◎Steps

1   Consider the type of invitation. If it came by phone or e-mail, chances are the party is casual. If you received a formal invitation, and especially if the event benefits a charity or association, consider it a dressier affair.

2   Think about the season. Wear lighter-weight fabrics and brighter colours for spring and summer get-togethers. Stick to dark, muted tones in heavier fabrics for autumn and winter gatherings.

3   Dress up casual business attire for a more formal after-work cocktail party. Add a blazer to chinos and a button-down shirt, or pair a sports jacket with black jeans and a black poloneck. Switch sandals or trainers for dark leather loafers or lace-up shoes.

4   Treat cocktail parties on weekend afternoons less formally than those scheduled in the evening. Go dressy business casual for a more formal late-afternoon gathering; opt for a suit in the evening. For a less formal event, wear a nice casual outfit in the afternoon and dressier business casual clothes in the evening.

✱Tips

Trainers and sports socks are inappropriate for a cocktail party. Shorts are also not advisable, even on summer afternoons. Opt for lightweight trousers in cotton or linen instead.

Check a formal invitation for terms like "semi-formal" or "black-tie optional". If you see these, a suit and tie is your best option.

Coordinate your outfit with your date's.

Style and Etiquette

Dress for a Cocktail Party – Women

Cocktail parties are the perfect occasion for the famous little black dress (see 146 "Buy a Perfect Little Black Dress"). Whatever your attire, keep it dressy and elegant, but not too formal.

Steps

1. Think about your invitation. If it came by phone or e-mail, the chances are it's a more casual affair. If you received a formal invitation, and especially if the event benefits a charity or association, consider it a dressier affair.

2. Choose dress and skirt lengths from mini to just above the ankles. Save anything resembling a full-length sequined gown for a different occasion.

3. Choose fabric according to the season. Wool and wool blends are perfect for autumn and winter; satin, silk, rayon and fine-gauge knits are great for the spring and summer. These materials can be dressed up or down with jewellery, handbags, shoes, shawls and hairstyles.

4. Attend a more formal after-work party in a business suit, or if you wear more casual clothes to work, bring an outfit to change into. A black woolen dress with stockings and slip-on shoes is a simple solution for autumn or winter. Pair a strapless or spaghetti-strap dress with an embroidered cardigan and slingbacks or strappy sandals for a spring or summer event.

5. Head to a more casual after-work gathering in a dressy-casual outfit. Pair a woolen skirt with a fitted poloneck and flat leather shoes for winter parties. Consider a fine-knit twinset, slim satin trousers and low-heeled backless shoes in the summer.

6. Wear a printed A-line sundress to a cocktail party on a weekend afternoon. A party scheduled for a weekend evening warrants a more flirty or elegant ensemble. Pair a colourful satin or silk empire-waist dress with a velvet or silk shawl.

7   Accessorise. Show off your gold charm bracelet or favourite pair of dangling earrings. Match hair adornments and a handbag to the motif, material or colours in your outfit.

❋ Tips

Colours such as grey, crimson, black, dark brown and dark blue flatter for evening, autumn and winter events. During the summer and spring, consider florals and seasonal shades like light pink, sky blue, pale green, pale yellow and other pastels.

Choose a dress that flatters your figure – don't squeeze into a dress that's too tight or low-cut.

149

Choose a High-Quality Garment

Check the quality of clothes before you spend your hard-earned money. The following is a quick rundown on the particulars of good craftsmanship.

◎ Steps

Fabric and Stitching

1   Inspect fabrics to make sure patterns line up at the seams – especially at the shoulders, collar and sewn-on (patch) pockets.

2   Hold fabric up to the light and make sure the weave is tight, even and uniform, with no loose or undone threads. If the fabric has beads or sequins, make sure they're securely attached.

3   Check the grain of the fabric. The vertical grain should run straight up and down the garment, and the horizontal grain should run at a 90-degree angle to this line.

4   Crumple heavier fabric, such as wool, to see if it bounces back, either immediately or in several minutes, indicating resistance to wrinkling.

5   Verify that all stitches are secure and straight. You should see about 8 to 12 stitches per 2.5 cm (1 in).

Examine hems, which should be nearly invisible. Hemmed bottoms should hang straight and not curl or pucker.

Other Details

1   Compare fabric lengths: fold trousers, shirts, skirts and other garments in half lengthwise to ensure that the right and left sides are symmetrical. Check that the right and left sides of the collar are equal in shape, size and positioning.

2   Confirm that patch pockets lie perfectly flat against the cloth, with no space between the pocket and the front of the garment. While holding the garment upright, make sure that the pocket doesn't hang away from the front.

3   Hold up clothing to ensure that the lining follows the cut of the garment, falls smoothly and does not extend below the hemline. In general, women's trousers are fully lined, while men's trousers are lined only in front to just below the knees.

4   Verify that buttons and buttonholes are sewn tightly, with no unravelled thread. In general, the more buttons a shirt has, the higher quality it is; spare buttons are an added plus.

5   Try on a shirt before buying it. Button it fully, making sure that buttons are placed well so that the shirt doesn't gape open across the chest.

6   Pull zips up and down a few times to make sure that they run smoothly and don't snag.

⚠ Warning

Take note of stains on a garment, particularly lipstick and other make-up marks around the neck area. If you notice a stain and still want to buy the item, find out if the store will dry-clean it, or ask for a discount. Alternatively, find out if you can get a refund if you can't remove the stain at home.

Choose High-Quality Shoes

You don't have to spend a fortune to buy well-made shoes
that fit comfortably – you just need to know what to look for.

◉ Steps

Ensuring Fit

1 Ask a sales assistant to measure both your feet, as right and left foot
sizes often differ slightly.

2 Try on shoes with socks of appropriate thickness – pop socks, thin
socks or athletic socks, depending on the type of shoe you're thinking
of buying.

3 Press on the shoe to locate your longest toe. You should feel at most
a thumb's width between your longest toe and the end of the shoe.

4 Walk several paces with the shoes on and feel how they fit around
your heels, insteps, toes and the ball of your foot.

5 Make sure the shoe doesn't scrape against your anklebone.

6 Keep in mind that shoes should feel comfortable from the start; don't
rely too much on "breaking them in" over time, despite what the sales
assistant may say.

Ensuring Quality

1 Examine the sole to make sure it is firmly attached to the shoe. Keep
in mind that some soles are glued to the upper shoe and others are
stitched. Either type is acceptable, and some shoes (mainly men's
shoes and trainers) will be both glued and stitched.

2 Check the heel. High-quality dress shoes have leather heels,
sometimes with a layer of rubber or nylon on the back edge of the
heel. Heels on high-heeled shoes for women are usually made of
plastic and covered with leather. The higher the price, the higher
quality the plastic.

3   Inspect the shoe's interior. Leather interiors absorb foot moisture best. Good-quality shoes are fully lined from front to back.

4   Consider the shoe material. Shoes with an oiled, natural finish are durable, while patent- and polished-leather shoes resist dirt. Suede shoes stain easily and need to be sprayed with a protectant.

5   Examine buckles and any adornments on the shoe. They should be securely attached and reinforced with even, smooth double stitching.

✳ Tips

When deciding on shoe size, consider the shoe material's ability to stretch. For example, calfskin stretches more than manufactured materials.

Shop for shoes in the late afternoon rather than the morning. Your feet may swell slightly over the course of the day.

Determining where the shoe is made can help you assess quality: Italian materials, design and assembly, for example, often indicate a shoe of high quality.

⚠ Warning

You should not find bits of glue anywhere on the shoe. This is especially true for trainers.

151

Buy a Diamond

Choosing a diamond involves more than a casual trip to the jewellers. Armed with the proper knowledge, you can make an informed decision and a wise investment.

◎ Steps

1   Decide how much you can spend. If you are buying an engagement ring, the general rule is two months' salary, but the sky's the limit if you're in pursuit of the perfect stone.

2   Choose the shape of diamond you prefer. Although the round, or brilliant, cut is most popular, diamonds come in many cuts, including oval, square or even heart-shaped.

3   Inspect the diamond's clarity (the degree of transparency). A "flawless" diamond, free from all inclusions or blemishes, is very rare. Other diamonds are rated on a clarity scale that grades diamonds from "flawless" to "obvious inclusions" – the higher the diamond's rating on this scale, the greater its value.

4   Examine the diamond's colour. Although you may not generally think of diamonds as having colour, some have a yellow, grey or brown cast. Pure, colourless diamonds are at the top of the colour scale. Diamonds are also available in "fancy" colours such as red, blue or purple. These diamonds are rare and more expensive than the normal clear to yellow variety.

5   Examine the diamond's cut, which is crucial to the brilliance of the stone and a major factor in its value. A well-cut diamond reflects and disperses light in beautiful ways, thanks to qualities such as symmetry and depth (the bottom of the diamond shouldn't be too shallow or too deep). Diamonds are graded according to the cut quality, and this grade should carry a great deal of weight in your decision.

6   Determine the weight, which is measured in carats. The greater the carat weight, the more valuable the diamond. Keep in mind that since larger stones are more rare, two $1/2$-carat diamonds are less expensive than a single 1-carat diamond.

7   Compare several diamonds side by side and get a good idea of what you can find in your price range. No two diamonds are alike, so examine all of them carefully for their unique qualities.

8   Make your final decision based on which diamond offers the best combination of the four C's: clarity, colour, cut and carat. Ignore any of these attributes, and you jeopardise your chances of getting the best diamond for your money.

✴ Tips

Enquire about a certificate from the Gemological Institute of America (GIA). The GIA, the largest impartial diamond-grading authority in the world, issues a grading report and details the diamond's specifications after examining it.

A nicked and scratched stone is almost certainly fake, but only a jeweller can detect some fakes. Have a questionable stone professionally appraised.

Buy from a jeweller who will guide you through the process. A good jeweller will help you assess how much you can spend, show you a wide selection of diamonds, and explain what to look for.

Buying a loose diamond gives you the option of designing a setting around the stone.

When buying a ring, opt for platinum or white gold: metals other than yellow or rose gold enhance the brilliance of the diamond due to their colour.

⚠ Warning

Don't try to get the largest possible diamond for your money. This can mean overlooking quality in favour of size and ending up with an inferior stone. Balancing all factors is the best approach to choosing a quality diamond.

152
Buy Pearls

Versatile and classic, pearls are a worthwhile investment that can soften a business suit or add more elegance to a dress. Here's what to look for.

◉ Steps

General Considerations

1   Decide whether you want natural, cultured or imitation pearls. Keep in mind that imitation pearls are costume jewellery and are of very little value; natural pearls are almost impossible to buy and often aren't as high in quality as cultured pearls.

2   Choose a pearl shape: round, symmetrical or baroque and/or irregular. Sphere-like round pearls are the most expensive and highly prized. Symmetrical pearls, such as those shaped like teardrops, should be evenly shaped.

3   Consider pearl size, the most important factor in price. The larger the pearl, the more it will cost.

4   Decide if you want a double-strand necklace of smaller pearls (cheaper) or a single strand of larger pearls (more expensive).

5   Place pearls directly under a light on a flat, white surface in order to inspect them.

6   Inspect each pearl for lustre. Lustrous pearls have a shiny surface, good contrast between light and dark areas, and strong, crisp reflections. Avoid pearls that resemble dull, cloudy white beads.

7   Look at the pearl's "orient", a play of iridescent rainbow colours – characteristic of high-quality pearls.

8   Examine pearl colour, which can be white, yellow, black, grey or various other colours. Ask whether the colour is natural or dyed; the latter is less expensive. More exotic natural colours are more expensive.

9   Inspect the pearl's "overtone", a tint secondary to the main body colour. Pinkish overtones can increase pearl price, while green or blue tints may lower the price.

10 Verify the pearl's cleanliness by checking that it has minimal surface blemishes such as nicks, cracks, pits or discoloration.

11 Turn the pearl in your hands to examine it from all angles. Colour, shape, smoothness and lustre all may vary within a single pearl. Roll a strand of pearls on a flat surface to test them for roundness – round pearls roll more smoothly and evenly.

Distinguishing Real Pearls From Imitations

1   Run the pearl lightly along the biting edge of your front teeth. A real pearl will feel slightly gritty or sandy, whereas a fake pearl will feel smooth. This is a standard test for authenticity that most sellers will allow, as long as you ask first.

2   Look at and feel the pearl. Absolutely flawless-looking pearls, as well as those that feel unusually light when you bounce them in your hands, are probably fake.

3   Examine the pearl under a 10X magnifier (a loupe). Imitation pearls appear grainy.

Natural pearls, which are rare and valuable, form when oysters reflexively coat a foreign particle with nacre. Cultured pearls start off with an artificially implanted bead nucleus that triggers the same response in the oyster. Imitation pearls are composed of glass or plastic.

The only certain way to distinguish between a natural and a cultured pearl is to have the pearl X-rayed.

If you're buying a pearl necklace, it should have a knot between each pearl to hold the necklace together in case the string breaks.

Compare a pearl with others in the same strand. Verify that pearls within a strand match in colour, tint and size. Comparing one strand of pearls with another might help you assess lustre and colour more accurately.

△ Warning

Pearls offered at unbelievably low prices are probably fake.

153

Clean Jewellery

Before cleaning your jewellery, examine it carefully to make sure that all settings, clasps and prongs are secure. Once you've done that, you're ready to proceed.

◎ Steps

Gold, Platinum and Gemstones

1   Use a non-abrasive jewellery cleaner, which you can purchase at a local jewellers. Or use a cleaning solution of mild soap and water.

2   Dip the jewellery in the cleaner or cleaning solution.

3   Rinse in warm running water.

4   Buff dry with a soft, lint-free cloth until it's shiny.

Silver

1 Clean the silver with a non-abrasive silver polish.

2 Apply the polish with a soft cloth, gently working it into stains.

3 Wipe away excess polish and buff the jewellery with a soft, lint-free cloth until it's shiny.

4 Keep in mind that frequently wearing silver jewellery can keep it from becoming tarnished.

✳ Tips

Store jewellery carefully to avoid damage. Sturdy cases with partitioned, soft interiors protect and organise items.

Jewellers recommend having jewellery professionally cleaned at least once a year.

⚠ Warnings

Do not use jewellery cleaner on pearls and porous stones, such as emeralds, rubies, lapis lazuli, coral and turquoise. Wipe them clean with a soft, damp cloth or have them cleaned professionally. Consult a jeweller when in doubt about a particular stone.

Exposure to perfume, cosmetics or perspiration can stain gemstones.

154

Retrieve a Valuable Dropped Down the Sink

Don't panic! Dropping something of value down the drain isn't always the nightmare it seems. Try this method to get it back.

◉ Steps

1 Turn off the water immediately to prevent the item being washed out of reach and put the plug in.

2 Open the cabinet beneath the sink.

Style and Etiquette

3 Find the trap – this is the U-shaped piece of pipe that connects the vertical pipe running from the sink to the horizontal pipe that goes into the wall.

4 Place a bucket under the trap.

5 Loosen the large threaded nuts that attach the trap to the other pipes. Sometimes you can do this with your hands; otherwise, you may need to use a large pair of pliers or even a plumber's pipe wrench.

6 Pull the trap away with a good yank, letting it fall into the bucket as necessary. Beware, the trap will be full of dirty water.

7 Put on gloves. Empty the trap into your hand – over the bucket – and look for your valuable.

8 Reassemble the trap, being careful not to overtighten the nuts.

❋ Tips

There may be another trap or filter in the main plumbing system, so if your valuable has already passed the sink trap, it may still be in the main trap. Call a plumber.

If you're afraid of stripping or damaging the nuts holding the plumbing together, place a thin rag or tape around the nuts before grabbing them with the plumber's wrench.

Things You'll Need

☐ bucket

☐ pliers or a plumber's wrench

☐ rubber gloves

Gain Weight

Gaining weight may be a cinch for most people, but for those who don't put on pounds easily, it can be a real struggle. Here's how to bulk up while maintaining a healthy lifestyle.

◎Steps

1. Eat nutritious foods that are high in calories. Some examples are whole-grain breads, avocados, potatoes, kidney beans, lean red meat, poultry and fish.

2. Boost the caloric value of your meals using healthy additions. Add powdered milk to casseroles, add avocados and olives to sandwiches, add wheat germ to cereal, add chopped meat to pasta sauce, and so on.

3. Eat three meals a day and at least two snacks.

4. Increase your normal portion size. Take a second scoop of pasta, or add a banana to your muesli.

5. Choose higher-calorie foods when given a choice. For example, sweetcorn is higher in calories than green beans.

6. Relax – excessive fidgeting and restlessness can burn up a lot of calories.

7. Add weight lifting to your exercise programme. It helps build muscle mass. Be aware, though, that this will speed up your metabolism, so you'll need to increase your calories even more.

8. Tally up your calorie intake, and compare it with the number of calories you're burning. You need to be taking in more than you use up, and you may need to ease up a little on your exercise programme.

✳ Tips

If you cannot seem to put on any weight, you should see a doctor to rule out any physical problems, such as hormonal imbalances.

Health and Fitness

Although it seems like a logical way to bulk up, avoid adding excess fat and sweets to your diet. Too much fat is bad for your health regardless of your weight, and filling up on junk food will keep you from getting all the nutrition you need from healthier foods. Eat fats and oils in moderation; they should account for no more than 30 per cent of your total calorie intake.

Consult your doctor before beginning any weight-gain programme.

156
Lose Weight

Proper diet and exercise can aid weight loss, as well as keeping you healthy. The challenge is to follow through. Others have lost weight by following these simple guidelines – so can you.

◎ Steps

1 Set small, realistic goals. Some good goals are to increase your exercise or activity by ten minutes, or to cut down on unhealthy snacks or canned drinks in the afternoon.

2 Start a regular exercise programme and stick with it. Aim for a minimum of 30 minutes, three or four times a week. You'll burn more calories and get fit faster if you exercise even more – 30 to 60 minutes, five to seven times a week.

3 Sneak in extra exercise in addition to your regular programme. Park at the far end of the car park and walk; take the stairs instead of the lift.

4 Eat low-fat, high-fibre foods such as salads and vegetable pasta dishes.

5 Choose foods that you like. Learn to prepare healthy, low-calorie foods that taste good. Eating well doesn't have to mean eating dull foods.

6   Eat smaller, more frequent meals. Some experts believe that this way, your body starts to increase its metabolism so that calories are burned faster. Also, mini-meals can prevent overeating later on. Keep in mind that this may not work for everyone – and remember that snacking on crisps or doughnuts is not going to shrink your waistline. Stick to healthy, low-calorie foods.

7   Drink a minimum of eight glasses of water per day – more if you are active. Water is critical for weight loss.

8   Plan ahead. Keep the fridge stocked with healthy food, and you'll be less likely to run out for high-calorie, high-fat junk food.

9   Keep a food diary. This will help you pinpoint where you can improve your eating habits.

10 Once you discover your favourite snack time, be sure to have plenty of healthy options available.

11 Make sure you've chosen an exercise programme you enjoy, and don't rule out the unconventional – regular vigorous dancing is exercise, too. Consult a doctor to find an exercise programme that is best for you if you are extremely overweight.

12 Lose weight gradually – you are more likely to keep it off. A safe amount is 0.5 to 0.75 kg (1 to 1½ lb) per week.

✳ Tips

Lose weight with a friend, or join a support group.

Avoid vending machines by carrying around your own healthy snacks.

⚠ Warning

Consult your doctor before beginning any weight-loss programme.

Fit Exercise Into Your Busy Schedule

Make a commitment to exercise every day if you can. Try to get in at least 30 minutes of walking or more vigorous exercise.

Steps

1. Try walking, cycling or roller-blading to work. If this takes longer than your usual commute, plan ahead: pack your briefcase and lay out your clothes the night before. Keep a change of clothes at work if need be.

2. If an alternative commute is impossible, get off the bus a little earlier and walk the rest of the way, park at the far end of the car park, or take the stairs instead of the lift.

3. Make use of your lunch break. Play a quick game of squash, make a speedy gym visit, go for a jog or take a brisk walk (use some light hand weights for a bonus workout).

4. Stretch at your desk. This reduces muscle tension, gets your circulation moving and prepares you for more strenuous activity later.

5. Do some chores. Mow the lawn or rake the leaves for 20 minutes. Housework burns calories, and you have to get the work done anyway.

6. Play games with your children. Kick a football or play some hopscotch.

Tips

New mums can join an aerobics class specially designed for them and their babies. You can network with other mums, stay fit and keep an eye on the baby, who gets involved as part of your workout routine.

Exercise with a friend – you can motivate one another.

Carry a notebook and keep a record of your activities and their duration. Increase your daily exercise as time goes on.

Warning

Always consult your doctor before beginning an exercise programme.

Stay Motivated to Exercise

You know you should exercise, but some days it's tough to get moving. Discover what motivates you, and use these strategies to develop and maintain an active lifestyle.

Steps

1 Determine an attainable goal, such as exercising twice during the week and once on weekends. Creating realistic goals will set you up for success. If your goal becomes too easy, you can always design a more ambitious one.

2 Devise rewards for achieving your goal. The reward can be a massage, a new workout outfit, a new CD, a session with a personal trainer or that hardcover novel you've had your eye on – whatever you really want.

3 Partner with a friend, co-worker or loved one – someone who will support you and your goals without sabotaging them.

4 Subscribe to a fitness magazine or online fitness newsletter. New tips and exercises can be inspirational and alleviate boredom.

5 Create a competition with co-workers or friends. For example, the team whose members exercise for 30 minutes, three times each week, for two months wins a prize.

6 Change into your workout clothes. Sometimes, just getting dressed is the biggest barrier.

7 Erase the concept that if you can't do at least 30 minutes you're wasting your time. Even in small doses, exercise burns calories, increases energy and improves your health.

8 Try a new sport or class. Adding variety, group support and competition can increase your likelihood of exercising.

9 Make a commitment to your dog or your neighbour's dog to go for a long walk at least twice each week.

10   Look for ways to incorporate activity into your day, even if you can't do your normal exercise routine. Take the stairs instead of the lift, go bowling instead of to the cinema, or use a push mower instead of a powered mower.

11   Sign up for a race and send in the entry fee. Whatever your activity – running, cycling, walking, swimming – there are hundreds of races offered all over the world. Pick a place you've always wanted to visit.

12   Join a gym or health club. For some, paying for a membership increases the likelihood of compliance. It also eliminates the bad-weather excuse.

☀ Tips

Exercise in the morning. Research shows that people who make exercise a priority first thing in the day are more likely to stick with it.

Every person goes through periods when it's very challenging to maintain an exercise programme. Acknowledge it when it happens, recognise that it's just a brief period of time, and restart your programme as soon as possible.

Choose things that motivate you – not what others want.

Remind yourself of the many health benefits of an exercise programme.

159
Meditate

Meditation can be calming, rejuvenating and restorative. When practised regularly, it can aid in reducing stress, lowering blood pressure and increasing personal awareness.

◎ Steps

1   Choose a tranquil location, free of distractions.

2   Decide whether you'd like to have soothing music in the background.

3   Select a comfortable chair or place to sit, and assume a sitting position with your spine relatively straight.

4   Close your eyes.

5   Breathe in, allowing your ribcage and belly to expand as you inhale.

6   Exhale slowly.

7   Concentrate on your breathing. Be aware of each breath and the feelings of deeper relaxation.

8   Allow thoughts and feelings to enter your mind. Acknowledge them, allow them to pass, and refocus on your breathing.

9   Open your eyes after you feel more relaxed and centred.

10   Begin with five to ten minutes of meditation each day and increase to 20 minutes or more twice each day.

✳ Tips

There are many forms and variations of meditation. If one particular form doesn't work for you, try another.

Avoid meditating on a full stomach. The best time to meditate is just before eating.

Some studies have suggested meditation may decrease the risk of heart disease, possibly because the resulting stress relief may promote the body's self-repair system to thin the fatty build-up on artery walls. Still, meditating should never be used as a substitute for a healthy diet, exercise and proper medical care.

160

Break a Bad Habit

Habits such as biting your nails, downing large amounts of caffeine and even gossiping are automatic behaviours that can be changed with patience and persistence.

◎ Steps

1   Decide how serious you are about breaking the habit. In addition to a strong commitment, you'll need time and energy to pay attention to your behaviour so you can change it.

2   Keep track of the behaviour. Keep a notepad or journal handy.

3   Write down when it happens (what the overall situation is when it occurs) and what you were thinking and feeling. Writing increases your awareness of when and why you have this habit.

4   Read and think about what you write down. What does this habit do for you? Is it a way to deal with feelings of boredom, anxiety, stress or anger?

5   Think of what you could do instead of the habit that would be a more positive way to deal with the feelings or situations that provoke it. Write down some simple alternative behaviours. Pick one you want to practise.

6   Try to catch yourself when you find yourself indulging in the habit, and stop yourself as soon as you can. Start the alternative behaviour you decided you wanted to do instead.

7   Aim to do this once a week at first, then increase the number of times per week over time. The more you practise a new behaviour, the more it becomes the new habit.

8   Get support from others by letting them know you are working on the habit and telling them what they can do to help.

❋ Tips

Be patient with yourself. Habits are so automatic and unconscious, you may not even realise you're engaging in the behaviour until you're already doing it.

Be kind to yourself. Browbeating yourself is another bad habit to be broken.

Stop Smoking

You've probably already heard the many reasons why you should stop smoking – now check out the various ways of how to go about it.

Steps

1 Ask yourself why you want to stop smoking.

2 Write your answers on a piece of paper and carry it with you.

3 Whenever you feel like smoking, use your list to remind yourself of why you want to stop.

4 Fill out a "stop smoking contract". Sign it, and have a family member or friend sign it as a witness.

5 Throw away all your cigarettes, lighters and ashtrays.

6 Change your schedule to avoid circumstances in which you usually smoke. Walk around the block or chew gum when you would normally be smoking.

7 Put up no-smoking signs in your house, your work area and your car.

8 Prepare yourself to feel the urge to start smoking again. Here are four ways to deal with the urge to smoke: delaying, deep breathing, drinking water and doing something else.

9 Carry around "mouth toys" – sweets, chewing gum, straws, carrot sticks.

10 List the good things that have happened since you stopped smoking, and keep the list with you as an inspiration wherever you go. For example, you might note that your breath is fresher, you can climb the stairs without losing your breath, and you've saved enough money to buy a new DVD player.

11 Reward yourself for stopping smoking; for example, you could take the money you have saved and buy yourself something nice.

Health and Fitness

Tips

Ask your doctor about nicotine products and other types of medication if you have tried unsuccessfully to stop in the past.

Be prepared to persist despite a few relapses.

Planning meals, eating a healthy diet and staying active will help you maintain your weight.

Look for a support group or smoking-cessation class.

Warning

You may experience irritability, depression or a dry mouth due to nicotine withdrawal after you stop smoking. These symptoms should pass.

162

Stop Worrying

The keys to worrying less are to challenge your worrisome thoughts and to calm yourself physically and emotionally.

Steps

1   Write down what you are worried about. Include your imagined worst-case scenarios.

2   Think about how you would handle your worst-case scenarios.

3   Decide what actions you could take that would change the situation and give you less to worry about. Then follow through on those actions.

4   Try to think logically about the worrisome thoughts that you feel you can't take any action on. Consider which of them are excessive or distorted and have very little basis in reality.

5   For each of these worrisome thoughts, write down an alternative way of looking at the problem that presents a rational challenge to your worries.

Self-Improvement

6   Try to catch yourself when you notice that you're becoming overwhelmed with worry. Stop and remind yourself of the alternative way to look at the situation.

7   Practise relaxation and stress-reduction techniques. One simple thing you can do to help quiet your mind and calm your emotions and body is to breathe in slowly and deeply to the count of six and breathe out slowly to the count of six. Do this for five minutes; gradually increase to 20 minutes over time.

8   Learn to accept what you cannot change or have no power to control in life. Read books dealing with worry, anxiety, acceptance and inner peace. Look in the psychology, self-help and spirituality sections of your bookshop or library.

✳ Tips

If you need to, get help from others in coming up with challenges to your worrisome thoughts. They can often present you with a different perspective on things.

Many people find spiritual teachings or belief in a higher power extremely helpful in decreasing worry and developing more trust in life.

⚠ Warning

Seek professional help if your worries are interfering with your daily functioning or causing you significant distress.

163

Create Your Own Package Holiday Using the Internet

The internet has opened up a world of possibilities for travellers. It offers direct access to hundreds of travel companies and makes it easy to shop around and get the best deal.

◎ Steps

1   Do an internet search for your desired destination combined with

Travel

the type of accommodation you would ideally like (such as cottage, villa, hotel).

2 Search also for the tourist office that is local to your destination (start with the tourist office for the country or region and narrow it down). Tourist office websites often have comprehensive listings and links. You may wish to send off for brochures either by e-mail or by phone and post to make your final selection.

3 Check transport to your destination. There are countless websites for air (scheduled and charter), train and ferry tickets, or you can arrange car hire over the web (and obtain route planning maps). Compare prices and travel times and decide on the best means of travel.

4 When you know when and how you want to reach your destination and where you want to stay, start making your booking, only confirming when all the pieces of your package are in place.

5 Send your payment over the internet if the site offers secure payment. Most sites also offer more traditional means of payment.

❋ Tip

Don't forget to organise your own travel insurance.

⚠ Warning

Check the credentials of a company before booking with with them. Reputable companies in the UK travel industry will be members of professional and regulatory bodies such as ATOL and ABTA.

164

Buy Cheap Air Tickets

With a little forethought and some flexibility, you can reach your favourite destinations without breaking the bank.

◎ Steps

1 Keep yourself updated on ticket prices by watching the news and reading the newspaper. Look for limited-time promotional fares from major airlines and airline companies just starting up.

2. Be flexible in scheduling your flight. Tuesdays, Wednesdays and Saturdays are typically the cheapest days to fly; late-night flights ("red-eyes"), very early morning flights and flights with at least one stop tend to be discounted as well.

3. Ask the airline if it offers travel packages to save money in other areas. For instance, is a hire car or hotel room available at a discount along with the air ticket?

4. Find out whether the stated fare is the cheapest, and enquire about other options when speaking to the airline reservations service. If you're using the internet, check more than one website and compare rates.

5. Enquire about stand-by fares if you're flying off-season. High season is a bad time to fly stand-by because most airlines overbook flights, making it difficult to find a spare seat.

6. Purchase tickets through consolidators (or "bucket shops"), who buy blocks of tickets and sell them at a discount to help an airline fill up all available seats.

7. Book early. You can purchase advance-ticket discounts by reserving 21 days ahead; book even earlier for summer holiday flights, especially in November and December. Keep in mind that holiday "blackout periods" may prevent you from using frequent-flier miles.

8. Stay with the same airline during your entire trip to receive round-trip or connecting fare discounts.

✱ Tips

Note strict refund and exchange policies on tickets bought through name-your-price sites.

Once you've shopped around, consult a travel agent to find out if he or she can ferret out a cheaper ticket.

See also 165 "Make the Most of Your Frequent-Flier Miles".

If you will be visiting different countries on the same trip, you can save by asking the agent to arrange flights in which you arrive in one city but depart from another.

Ask about student and pensioner discounts.

Travel

Consolidators may delay in delivering your tickets, don't allow refunds or exchanges, and don't take reservations. To protect yourself, purchase through a travel agent, pay by credit card, and consider buying travel-cancellation insurance.

165

Make the Most of Your Frequent-Flier Miles

Flying can earn you frequent-flier miles, as can putting purchases on a credit card with an airline tie-in. After all that spending, don't waste those precious miles – learn the tricks for using them.

◎ Steps

1. Choose one frequent-flier programme and concentrate on maximising your benefits within that programme.

2. Know and use the frequent-flier programme's partners, who may range from florists to telephone companies to hotels.

3. Consult the programme's newsletter frequently for updates on new partners and promotions. If you don't receive the newsletter by post, call and request a subscription, or check online for newsletter postings.

4. Keep track of your miles. Work towards attaining elite status if you are a high-frequency traveller, or a free trip if you are a leisure traveller.

5. Save your free miles for flights that are usually expensive.

6. Check your statements carefully, and keep your travel receipts in case the airline forgets to credit your account properly.

✳ Tip

Purchase tickets using frequent-flier miles as early as possible – even a year in advance if you can. These tickets get snapped up quickly.

Transport

Choose a Good Seat on an Aeroplane

Where should you sit on an aeroplane if you're prone to motion sickness? If you have a connecting flight? If you're travelling with kids? Ask an airline agent about reserving the right seat for you.

Steps

1 Request bulkhead seats – those behind the dividing walls of a plane – or a seat by one of the emergency exits if you want more leg room.

2 Choose an aisle seat for easier access to the overhead storage compartment and lavatories, as well as for faster disembarking.

3 Consider sitting near the lavatories if you are travelling with children.

4 Opt for the back of the plane if you want to spread out; there are usually fewer people in the back.

5 Sit towards the front if you want to get off the plane faster, which could be important if you're trying to make a tight connection. The front of the plane also tends to be a quieter ride.

6 Choose a seat toward the wings, which are the stability point for the plane, if motion sickness is a potential problem.

7 Sit near the galleys if you want early snack, drink or meal service.

Tips

If you're travelling with a companion, reserve the aisle and window seat of a three-seat row. Because middle seats are the last to be sold, you have a good chance of having an extra seat.

Join a frequent-flier programme to increase your chances of getting a good seat on the plane.

Warning

Exit-door seats must be filled by passengers willing and able to help people in an emergency and may not be available for reservation. Check with your airline agent.

Travel

Choose a Cruise

Cruise lines, one of the fastest-growing sectors of the travel industry, offer a wide variety of interesting destinations and activities for all ages.

Steps

1. Deal with a cruise-only travel agent or an online agency that specialises in cruise holidays. They are more likely to have access to special offers and cruise deals.

2. Decide where and when you want to cruise and the port you want to embark from. There are Caribbean and Asian sailings nearly year-round. Most cruises in Europe take place only in the summer, as do Alaskan cruises. Trips through the Panama Canal take place in spring and autumn.

3. Decide who will be joining you on the cruise. Families have different needs and entertainment requirements to single travellers or couples.

4. Outline the activities that appeal to you: ports of call, shore excursions, on-board facilities and amenities.

5. Decide if you have a preference about ship size. Large ships have more entertainment choices, while small ships have a more personal approach to service.

6. Determine your budget. Cruise lines give discounts for early bookings. You can also affect your costs by altering cruise dates, the length of your cruise and the region you sail to.

7. Ask about the typical age group of those sailing on a particular line or ship. This can help you determine whether you'll be compatible with your fellow passengers.

8. Choose the level of formality you prefer. Some ships demand formal or business attire at certain dinners. Other ships cater for holiday-makers who want to wear only casual clothing.

Be aware that port fees are often not included in advertised prices. They can add significantly to your cruise costs.

Budget for tips to waiters, room stewards and service personnel on board. Ships often have suggested amounts, depending on the length of the cruise.

Travel light. Getting on and off ships is not as easy as picking up your luggage at the airport.

Bring along toiletries, film and sunscreen. They can be quite expensive on board.

168

Avoid Over-packing

Moderation is key when packing for any trip. A good rule of thumb is to pack approximately half of what you initially think you're going to need.

Steps

1 Know your itinerary. If you know about the dressy events, casual evenings and business days you have in store, you can plan accordingly and avoid bringing unnecessary outfits.

2 Research the weather at your destination. If dry weather is expected, take a risk and skip the umbrella; if nighttime temperatures are known to plummet, pack layers for warmth.

3 Plan your clothes around one main coordinating colour. Black and khaki are good, neutral "foundation" colours that you can dress up, dress down, add colour to and accessorise for different events and different days. Consider bringing dark colours and prints that don't show the dirt.

4 Choose clothes for lightness and washability. Select several light layers that pack down easily and dry quickly, should you need to do

hotel-room washing. Avoid bulky items like sweaters and heavy coats if you can be comfortable in two to three interchangeable layers.

5   Pack a couple of favourite scarves or belts for variety.

6   Pack a bum bag or small backpack for day trips. If you're planning to shop, pack a lightweight holdall.

7   Wear your bulkiest outfit while travelling to save space in your luggage.

❋ Tips

Even if travelling for several months, you should never need more than five or six days' worth of clothing.

Check with your airline regarding restrictions on size, weight and number of pieces of luggage allowed.

For more comfortable travelling, each bag should weigh no more than 9 kg (20 lb) when fully packed.

169
Travel Crease-Free

To avoid looking creased and crinkled while you're on the road, buy and pack clothes in fabrics that resist crumpling – or that at least look good even when they're a bit rumpled.

◎ Steps

1   Buy clothes made of wool or silk. These natural fibres have some elasticity, which keeps them from crinkling.

2   Buy clothes made of synthetic fabrics or clothes that contain blends of synthetic and natural fibres. These fibres make clothing less crease-prone, more durable and easier to care for.

3   Opt for linen, which creases easily but "falls out" nicely and carries off the crumpled-casual look well.

4   Choose knits instead of woven fabrics. Knitwear – which includes cable, ribbed, tricot and jersey knits – creases less than woven fabrics.

5   Pack intelligently. Make use of flat suitcase pockets and special packing accessories that hold clothes in place, and don't overstuff your bags. Consider rolling knitwear, denims and linens to avoid harsh fold lines.

6   Unpack your bags upon arrival.

✳ Tips

Synthetics include nylon, polyester, microfibres, lycra, acrylic and acetate.

Cotton, like linen, is a natural fibre that creases easily (although the crumpled cotton look isn't generally in vogue). If you arrive at your destination with a few creases, hang up the clothes in the hotel bathroom while you run a steamy shower – harsh creases should fall out.

Besides your regular clothes and toiletries, you'll need to include articles appropriate to your particular holiday plans. Use the checklist below as your guide to four popular types of travel excursions.

Beach

- [ ] bathing suit
- [ ] sandals
- [ ] sunscreen and lip balm
- [ ] aloe vera gel for sunburn
- [ ] hat with a wide brim to protect your face
- [ ] sunglasses with adequate UV protection
- [ ] large towel, thin enough to fit into your beach bag
- [ ] refillable water bottle
- [ ] beach toys that fit easily into a bag, such as inflatable balls and Frisbees
- [ ] long-sleeved overshirt
- [ ] thin pair of long trousers
- [ ] long dress for cover-up
- [ ] reading material

Boat

- [ ] jacket
- [ ] rain jacket or foul-weather gear
- [ ] woolen socks
- [ ] waterproof shoes with non-slip soles
- [ ] gloves
- [ ] hat
- [ ] sunglasses
- [ ] sunscreen and lip balm
- [ ] binoculars
- [ ] still or video camera in waterproof bag
- [ ] seasickness medication (check with your doctor)
- [ ] life jacket
- [ ] navigation charts and guidebooks

checklist

Ski slopes

- [ ] thermals or undergarments made from polypropylene or a similar synthetic fibre
- [ ] polonecks and light sweaters
- [ ] heavy-duty ski jacket
- [ ] thin fleece jacket
- [ ] ski hat
- [ ] waterproof trousers
- [ ] goggles or sunglasses with adequate UV protection
- [ ] scarf
- [ ] gloves or mittens
- [ ] earmuffs or headband
- [ ] sunblock and lip balm
- [ ] several pairs of woolen and liner socks
- [ ] refillable water bottle

Outdoor activities

- [ ] sports bra
- [ ] three or four pairs of easy-to-wash trousers
- [ ] poloneck or other warm shirt
- [ ] warm jacket
- [ ] vest
- [ ] rain jacket
- [ ] thick woolen socks
- [ ] broken-in boots
- [ ] hat
- [ ] gloves
- [ ] sunglasses and sunhat
- [ ] sunscreen and lip balm
- [ ] maps and guidebooks

checklist

Travel

Make a Hotel Reservation

Comfortable and convenient places to stay – whether in a large hotel or a small bed-and-breakfast – will make your trip more pleasant. Here's how to arrange them without using a travel agent.

⊙ Steps

1 Buy a travel guide to your destination, especially if you're not familiar with the area. Read up on accommodation options and areas where places to stay are plentiful.

2 Plan your arrival and departure dates. If possible, choose off-season dates when you may be able to save money on accommodation.

3 Choose the area you want to stay in. This generally depends on where you will be doing business or on the recreational or cultural sights you want to see.

4 Find two or three hotels in your price range that appeal to you.

5 Call each hotel. Tell them the dates you will be lodging there and your room requirements, and ask for the room rate. Ask about family packages where kids stay for free or at a substantial discount, and about special deals that give you a discount on surrounding attractions.

6 Find out what other services are included in the room rate. Is a hot breakfast included? Afternoon tea?

7 Ask about any special rates that are available. For example, if you stay 4 nights during the low season, are you entitled to a special long weekend rate? If you adjust your dates slightly, can you get a better deal? Be sure the adjustment will be reflected in the final room rate.

8 Compare room rates and services and book one of the hotels. Be sure to specify a smoking or non-smoking room.

9 Reserve the room with your credit card. This will generally hold the room for you no matter what time you arrive.

You can also request a guide to places to stay from the tourist office of the area you'll be visiting. Remember, though, that you may get more honest appraisals from an independent guidebook, from friends' recommendations or from various websites.

If you are arriving at a local airport, ask if the hotel provides free transport from the airport to the hotel.

Ask about other extras that may be important to you: fridge, hair dryer, iron, gym, on-site restaurant, swimming pool, video, film rental, wheelchair access, pet-friendly facilities.

⚠ Warning

Check the hotel's cancellation policy. These differ from hotel to hotel, but if you cancel without letting the hotel know within the specified time, you may have to pay for a night's accommodation.

172

Get a Hotel-Room Upgrade

Sometimes upgrading your hotel room is possible, and sometimes it's not. Your chances depend on a combination of the available space, your arrival time and luck.

◎ Steps

1. Establish loyalty by always choosing the same hotel in cities you visit often. Being friendly with the reception staff never hurts.

2. Ask about freebies and other special deals when you book your reservation. If you don't ask, you usually don't get.

3. Join frequent-visitor programmes at the chain hotels you visit. Your points earn upgrades and free stays along with other perks.

4. Organise reunions, meetings or conferences at your favourite hotel. Lots of hotels say thanks with credit for upgrades or free nights, either at the time of the event or at a later date.

 Travel

5   Trade airline frequent-flier points for upgrades at participating hotels. But weigh this option carefully – it's rarely the most cost-effective way to spend frequent-flier points.

6   Be vocal. If the room you were assigned isn't satisfactory – dirty, noisy or lacking the view you were promised – ask for an upgrade.

7   Offer to be appeased. If the staff makes a mistake that causes a delay or distress – say they misplace your luggage or, in a worst-case scenario, fail to make your room safe – make it known that an upgrade will help you forget all about the bad experience.

8   Take a chance on luck. Once in a while, you'll be in the right place at the right time. Budget rooms sometimes get overbooked, and the lucky guest who gets bumped up to the executive floor could turn out to be you.

❋ Tip

Friendliness and charm may help encourage a hotel receptionist to go the extra mile for you.

173
Prevent Jet Lag

Jet lag doesn't have to ruin the first few days of your trip abroad. A few simple tips will help keep it in check.

◎ Steps

1   Start shifting your sleep-wake cycle to match that of your destination several days before departure, changing at the rate of one hour per day.

2   Begin adjusting to the time zone of your destination by resetting your watch at the beginning of your flight.

3   Sleep on the plane when it is night-time at your destination. Earplugs, headphones and an eye mask can help diminish noise and light.

4   Stay awake on the plane when it is daytime at your destination. Read a thriller with the light on and the window shade open, or walk around.

5   Drink plenty of water. The air on planes is extremely dry, and dehydration can worsen the effects of jet lag.

6   Avoid alcohol and caffeine while flying. They increase dehydration.

7   Exercise as much as you can on the flight during waking hours: stretch, walk down the aisles and do leg lifts.

Things You'll Need

❏ earplugs

❏ headphones

❏ eye mask

174

Treat Jet Lag

Flying across numerous time zones can affect travellers for days. Try the following tips to speed up the adjustment process.

◎ Steps

Daytime Arrival

1   Reset your watch to local time if you haven't done so already.

2   Eat a protein-packed breakfast, such as an omelette, which will help you stay awake.

3   Soak up natural sunlight to cue your body that it is time to be awake. Or spend your first day in well-lit places.

4   Get some exercise, but don't overdo it; a good option is a gentle walk outside during the day to get fresh air and keep your body moving.

Travel

5. Take a short nap if you are really weary, but do so before 2 pm and sleep for no longer than an hour.

6. Go to bed at a reasonable time. Even if you feel like dropping off at 5 pm, try to hold out until at least 8 or 9 pm so that you won't wake up too early the next morning.

Night-time Arrival

1. Eat a high-carbohydrate meal, such as pasta, to help make you drowsy.

2. Plan to go to bed at the local bedtime, even if you aren't sleepy.

3. Think about other ways to induce sleep: a hot bath with lavender oil, a cup of chamomile tea or a massage. Keep lights dim.

4. Avoid sleeping late, even if you did not sleep well.

✳ Tip

Make sure your hotel room is not too hot. You'll get the best night's sleep in a cool (but not cold) room.

⚠ Warnings

Avoid drinking alcohol to help you sleep. It will interfere with your body's natural sleep patterns. Also avoid drinking a lot of caffeinated drinks to keep yourself awake during the day. These will dehydrate you and make you more tired when they wear off.

Avoid driving, especially in an unfamiliar place, if you are overtired. If you must drive while weary, be very careful. Keep the window open and make frequent stops to keep sleepiness at bay.

Plan a Round-the-World Trip

A round-the-world trip is many people's dream, whether they are on a gap year or well into retirement. Plan carefully for the trip of a lifetime.

◎ Steps

1 Give yourself time to research your trip and your route before you set off.

2 Know yourself. Do you thrive on sponaneity or surprises or do you like to have a good idea of what's coming next? The answer will affect how you plan your trip. If you like order and organisation, you can plan a detailed schedule. Otherwise, you might be better off with a few key stops and time inbetween to wander off and explore.

3 List your must-see places and decide how long you would like in each.

4 Research the weather in the places you want to go, but don't get obsessed with it. You're not likely to be able to go to each place at the best time of year, but you can plan to avoid monsoons or deep winters.

5 Start to put together an itinerary. Decide whether you want to travel westwards or eastwards. Some websites offer a planning service.

6 Look into different flight deals. Some round-the-world tickets are offered by single airlines, and some by groups of airlines. All have different restrictions such as whether you can backtrack or how many stopovers you can have. You might have to accept some limits to get a cheaper deal.

7 Firm up your route to match the ticket deal you have chosen.

✳ Tips

Be realistic about your budget. Your ticket is the major expense, but ensure you have enough funds for the rest of the trip, too.

Travel

If you can only travel at a certain time of year, consider planning your trip around the places that are best during those months. Otherwise you may end up at your dream destination but at the worst time to see it.

Travel light, taking clothes with more than one use, such as trainers that can be rugged in the hills and the cities or thermal tops that are warm yet also light and easy to wash.

Keep up to date with world events in case they affect your route. No matter how much planning you've done, stay flexible.

176

Time Your Trip to Sydney

Sydney is a great destination year-round. It's a cosmopolitan, fun-loving city offering beaches, museums and galleries and plenty of open green spaces.

Steps

1. Decide when you want to visit. Seasons are the opposite of those in the northern hemisphere. Summer is from December to February and winter is from June to August. The average winter low is about 16°C (61°F) and the average summer high is about 26°C (79°F).

2. Book well ahead if you want to come for Christmas. December is peak season for getting to Sydney, with air tickets at their most expensive. It's a great time to visit, though, with barbecues on the beach and, throughout January, the Sydney festival, which ends with Australia Day on 26 January, and the Tall Ships race in Sydney Harbour.

3. Visit at the end of summer and start of autumn to see and participate in two of Sydney's major community events: the Gay and Lesbian Mardi Gras in February and March, and the St Patrick's Day parade on 17 March (or the previous Sunday).

4. Don't miss the Sydney Film Festival (in mid-June) if you like movies. More active visitors can watch or join in the City to Surf race on the second Sunday in August.

5   Join in with a national obsession and come for the rugby. In September there are both Rugby League and Rugby Union finals. Book early.

 Tips

At any time of year, you won't want to miss major sights like the Sydney Opera House, the Royal Botanic Gardens and the Art Gallery of New South Wales. For harbourside colour, shops and restaurants, visit The Rocks, and for speciality galleries and boutiques in small-scale streets of Victorian houses, visit the suburb of Paddington.

The Sydney Tower in the city centre offers amazing views over the city and beyond.

177

Time Your Trip to Thailand

With its amazing mix of frenetic urban life, awe-inspiring temples and laid-back beaches, Thailand offers an unparalleled range of experiences for the visitor.

⊙ **Steps**

1   Visit in the cool season of November to February, when there is less rain than at other times and it is not too hot, with an average temperature of about 27°C (80°F). The climate varies hugely around the country, and it's often better in the south in March to May, when the north is steaming hot – up to 33°C (91°F). The monsoon is from June to October.

2   The peak months for tourism are December and August – prices may be higher and it will certainly be more crowded.

3   Thai New Year is celebrated with the Songkran Festival in mid-April. A family affair, it involves bathing Buddhas and generally throwing water around in the streets – prepare to get soaked.

4   Rice festivals are important in rural life. In mid-May the Ploughing Ceremony marks the start of the rice planting. Between September and May there are local celebrations for the rice harvest.

 Travel

5 After the rainy season (usually in November) comes the lovely Loi Krathong Festival in which hundreds of candle-lit floats shaped as flowers are sent along the waterways for good luck.

6 Shoppers might like to visit Bangkok between mid-November and mid-December when shops hold a Grand Sale with up to 80 percent off everything. But within this period avoid the King's Birthday, 5 December, when the city is heaving with celebrating crowds.

✳ Tips

In Bangkok don't miss Wat Phra Kaew and the Grand Palace, and Wat Traimit (the Temple of the Golden Buddha). Jim Thompson's House is a peaceful collection of Thai art and architecture.

Beyond the capital, head for the second city of Chiang Mai in the north, and the Ayuthaya complex of temples and ruins, also north of Bangkok.

The most renowned islands are Ko Samui and Phuket.

⚠ Warning

Avoid the borders with Burma and Cambodia, where there may be bandits who pose a risk to travellers and others.

178
Time Your Trip to New York City

What other city has the audacity to style itself "the capital of the world"? New York is a city of superlatives, a kaleidoscope of famous buildings, museums and colourful neighbourhoods.

◎ Steps

1 Remember that late spring and early autumn bring the best weather to New York. Summers are often sweltering and humid, while snowfall and freezing temperatures are common during winter. The average July high is 29°C (84°F); the average January low is -3°C (26°F).

2 If food is your passion, don your trousers with the elastic waistband in mid-May and eat your fill of exotic fare at the International Food Fair on Ninth Avenue.

Destinations

3 Listen to the greatest musicians in jazz at the JVC Jazz Festival during the second half of June. About 300 artists play 40 venues in and around the city.

4 Celebrate the end of summer by joining the million-plus people who participate in the Caribbean Day parade on Labor Day, in Brooklyn.

5 Catch the latest arrivals to the silver screen at the New York Film Festival, held at Lincoln Center from late September to early October.

6 Cheer on runners at the New York City Marathon in early November. It's the largest in the United States and one of the most prestigious events of its kind worldwide. Two million cheering spectators line the course, along with 40-plus musical bands.

7 If you can bear the cold weather, experience the Christmas season New York–style by ice-skating in Rockefeller Plaza and by shopping among show-stopping window displays along Fifth Avenue and the designer boutiques along Madison Avenue.

8 Find out in advance about special exhibitions that may be coming to New York's world-class museums, which include the Metropolitan Museum of Art (the Met), the American Museum of Natural History, the Guggenheim Museum and the Museum of Modern Art (MOMA).

9 For good deals on tickets to Broadway and off-Broadway shows, stop by the TKTS (cut-price tickets) booth at the northern end of Times Square before afternoon or evening performances.

❋ Tips

New York is in a perpetual state of tourist high season. You stand the best chance of finding lower hotel rates and airfares from January to March, although even during these months it's difficult.

To find out what cultural events are going on, check out listings in *The Village Voice* weekly newspaper or the weekly magazines *New York* or *The New Yorker*.

No matter when you visit, make sure to ascend the Empire State Building and the Statue of Liberty, which afford great views of New York City but usually involve queuing. When you need to regain your sanity, take a daytime stroll in Central Park.

⚠ Warning

While recent years have definitely seen a decline in crime, visitors should

Travel

nonetheless observe the precautions they would in any large city, keeping personal valuables well secured and avoiding secluded or unsavoury-seeming areas after dark.

179

Time Your Trip to San Francisco

Scenic, colourful and tolerant, San Francisco offers something for everyone. Its location between the ocean and the bay makes the weather as unusual as the city itself.

◎ Steps

1. For the best weather, visit in May, September or October, but remember that gorgeous weather is possible any day of the year. The climate can change dramatically from moment to moment, and it even varies from neighbourhood to neighbourhood. June, July and August are often cold and foggy, suitable only if you're trying to escape from somewhere hot.

2. Take in the Chinese New Year Festival and Parade in late January or early February. The parade is one of the biggest nighttime illuminated processions in the country, and features floats, Chinese acrobats, a 60 m (200 ft) long dragon and lion dancers.

3. Check out the San Francisco Flower and Garden Show in mid-March to see how the visions of Bay Area landscapers reach fruition. Attend free seminars on various aspects of gardening.

4. Learn about Japanese culture – martial arts, tea ceremonies and singular food – at the Cherry Blossom Festival in late April.

5. If you are a film buff, don't miss the San Francisco International Film Festival, which runs from mid-April into early May. Well-respected throughout the world, the festival screens a variety of films, puts on gala opening and closing nights, and includes lots of glitzy parties for attendees and stars.

6   Jog from San Francisco Bay across the city to the Pacific Ocean. The Bay to Breakers, on the third Sunday in May, is a race with so many thousands of eccentrics that it feels more like a parade.

7   Fly your rainbow in June, the month San Francisco's gay community celebrates its freedom. There's a film festival, Gay Pride Week and a Gay Freedom Day parade.

8   Hit the North Beach Festival in June if you are a big fan of Italian and/or Beat culture. You can hear everything from opera to poetry readings and feast upon some of the city's best Italian cuisine.

9   Attend the San Francisco Blues Festival in late September. Always extremely popular, and a San Francisco favourite for almost 30 years, the festival includes world-class blues headliners playing at Fort Mason's Great Meadow.

10 Take your favourite chocoholic to the Ghirardelli Square Chocolate Festival, held in early September at the landmark Fisherman's Wharf headquarters of the famed local chocolate company. Sample all kinds of yummy treats like chocolate cheesecake and chocolate-covered strawberries.

11 Check out the fun at Fleet Week, a salute to sailors and the sea held in early October. You can watch the parade of ships, see Blue Angels air shows, tour ships or mingle with sailors to your heart's content.

✳ Tip

No matter what time of year you visit, make sure to take in a panoramic view of this spectacular city. Drive or walk up to Twin Peaks, a small double-tipped mountain sitting in the middle of San Francisco. Other good places from which to admire city views are the top of the Mark Hopkins Hotel on Nob Hill, Coit Tower in North Beach and the Golden Gate Bridge, which you can walk across.

⚠ Warnings

Summer is the season when travellers might wish to avoid San Francisco. Attractions are overrun by tourists, prices are higher, and the weather is often cold and foggy.

Rainy weather and poor visibility can cause significant delays at San Francisco International Airport. Find out if your airline flies into Oakland Airport just across the bay, which is often a better alternative.

Travel

Time Your Trip to Tokyo

Tokyo is so built-up and energetic, it makes New York feel like a lazy Sunday in the suburbs. Despite this intensity the Japanese are hospitable and helpful to strangers.

◎ Steps

1. Enjoy Tokyo's fairly temperate climate, which has four distinct seasons. Winter brings cold, sunny weather and the occasional snowfall. Spring and autumn are usually pleasant. June and early July are often rainy. Summer is hot and humid. The average July high is 27°C (80°F), and the average January low is 2°C (35°F).

2. Visit during April to pack numerous cultural events into one trip. The Buddha's birthday is celebrated nationwide on 8 April, and the cherry blossom season (Sakura Matsuri) is during the same month.

3. Take the train to the medieval capital of Kamakura for a spectacular festival honouring heroes of the Middle Ages; it's held at the Tsurugaoka Hachimangu Shrine on the second to the third Sunday in April. Head to Kanayama Shrine in the city of Kawasaki in mid-April for the Jibeta Matsuri, a festival praising the wonders of fertility.

4. Watch nearly naked giants wrestle. Most sumo matches in Tokyo are held in January, May and September, although you can see them on TV almost year-round.

❋ Tip

No matter when you go to Tokyo, make sure to visit the grand old Tokyo National Museum to learn about all aspects of Japanese civilisation through thousands of artifacts. Attend a performance of kabuki, ornate and easy-to-follow stage plays that have historically been the favourite form of entertainment in Japan. Asakusa (old Tokyo), the Tsukiji Fish Market and Roppongi, Tokyo's club district, are also popular.

⚠ Warning

Tokyo is the world's most expensive destination, estimated to be at least 60 percent more costly than New York.

Hit a Forehand in Tennis

Are your forehand ground strokes not making it over the net? Add zip to this most common of tennis shots. These directions are for right-handers; reverse them for left-handers.

Steps

1. Position yourself just inside the court's baseline and near the centre line.

2. Keep your feet shoulder-width apart.

3. Hold the racket at about waist level directly in front of you. Use the handshake grip, which works well for beginners. This grip is like shaking hands with the handle of your racket, while the string face is perpendicular to the court surface.

4. Bend your knees slightly. You should be able to feel some strain on the quadriceps muscles in your thighs.

5. As the ball is hit towards you, turn your shoulders to the right, pulling the racket back. Lower the racket head towards the playing surface. This should be done prior to the ball's crossing the net.

6. Pivot on your right foot. With your other foot, step forwards and across your body. Plant your left foot at a 45-degree angle, pointed towards the right net post.

7. Stop your backswing when the racket head is slightly below waist level and your arm is extended and relaxed. The racket, and your arm, should be perpendicular to the net so your arm and racket are pointing directly towards the back of the court.

8. Before the ball reaches you, pause for a moment, holding the racket in the backswing position. Think: "Bounce, step, hit".

9. Begin your swing from a position below your waist. Swing through the ball, with the contact occurring in front of your net-side hip. Try to hit the ball on the sweet spot (middle area) of the racket. This gives you a solid forehand by maximising the efficiency of the shot.

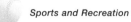

10 Finish the swing above the opposite shoulder. Think: "Start low, finish high".

11 Quickly get back into your original position for the next shot.

182

Hit a Backhand Ground Stroke in Tennis

The backhand ground stroke (turning 180 degrees to hit on the opposite side of your racket) is an essential tennis skill. Reverse the following alignments if you're left handed.

◉ Steps

1 Move from the ready position, pulling the racket across your body and back to the left-hand side before the ball crosses the net.

2 Keep your right hand loose on the grip.

3 Tuck the racket towards the inside of your body while dropping the racket head.

4 Step forwards with your right foot as you dip your right shoulder to the front, towards the net.

5 Swing from low to high, making contact when the ball is in front of your right hip, and finish above your right shoulder.

6 Help your playing arm during the shot by pointing the racket at the ground just before contact, then use your non-playing hand to grab

the throat of the racket and pull upward after contact as you turn your shoulders.

 Tips

Take small steps to position yourself after getting to the ball.

Tightening your forearm can cause pain in the wrist and elbow. Let the racket head do the work for you.

183

Hit a Golf Ball

Hitting a golf ball is easy, but hitting the ball where you want it to go takes a lot of practice. These instructions were written with right-handed hitters in mind; reverse them for left-handers.

◎ **Steps**

1 Stand behind the ball and pick out your target far up the fairway or driving range.

2 Check you are gripping the club properly.

3 Stand facing the ball with both feet together, about three-quarters of an arm's length away from the ball. Your left shoulder will be towards the target.

4 Take a tiny step towards your target (to the left) with your left foot, and take a normal step backwards (away from the ball) with your right foot. Your feet should now be shoulder-width apart.

5 Place your hands in a position known as the forward press. Viewed from above, this moves your hands slightly to the left of the ball. This angles the club forward (viewed from behind you, the shaft is now tilted to the left), flattening its already angled hitting face.

6 Pull the club to your right (straight back from the golf ball) to the top of the backswing. The club should be parallel to the ground, and back over your shoulder.

7 Without pausing at the top of the backswing, immediately swing the golf club back down along the same path.

8 Keep your head down and strike the ball. Allow the club to follow through until it touches your back.

9 Watch the ball travel towards the target.

 Tips

Don't be afraid to hit down on the ball and create a divot (a chunk taken out of the turf). Many people only catch the top of the ball, causing it to skip off down the fairway; this is because they do not dig deep enough. Replace the divot after your shot.

Remember that the harder you hit down, the higher it will go.

⚠ **Warnings**

Swinging the club too hard and too fast may cause back pain from all the furious twisting motion.

Make sure nobody is standing close to you when you swing a golf club.

184

Calculate Your Golf Handicap

Your handicap measures how well you'd stand up to a scratch golfer on any given course and allows golfers of different abilities to compete fairly.

◉ **Steps**

1 Take the scores from the last five rounds (18 holes each) you played.

2 For each of these scores look up the rating and slope for the course you played. This information is usually printed on the scorecard, although you can also get the rating and slope by calling the course.

3 Subtract the course rating from the score you earned on that course.

4 Multiply that number by 113. The resulting number is the differential.

5 Take the lowest of your five differentials and multiply it by 0.96, and you have your handicap.

 Tips

If you have seven or eight scores to use instead of five, average your two lowest differentials and then multiply by 0.96. If you have nine scores, average the three lowest differentials and multiply the result by 0.96.

Once you have 20 or more scores, use the most recent 20 scores and average the 10 lowest differentials; multiply the result by 0.96 to get your handicap.

185

Begin a Running Programme

Running will improve your stamina, help you control your weight and improve your general health. Here's how to get started.

◎ Steps

1　Jog before you run. Every running programme, no matter what level, has some jogging.

2　Begin at a conversational pace – one that allows you to talk comfortably without being winded.

3　Mix running with walking, if necessary. As you progress, increase the amount of running and decrease the walking.

4　Be patient with your initial aches and lack of stamina. Understand that although the heart and lungs grow strong quickly with exercise, muscles and joints take longer.

5　Increase your running time or distance by no more than 10 per cent each week to minimise the risk of injuries.

6　Build up your running to at least 20 to 30 minutes three times a week, done at a moderate level of intensity. Studies have shown that this is a sufficient amount of exercise for basic cardiovascular fitness. Running more than this amount is done for reasons beyond basic fitness.

7　Use the first month to learn about yourself. Pay close attention to your body; learn to read its signals of fatigue and stress, and when you can push beyond them.

❋ Tip

Find a partner or group. This will strengthen your commitment to a running programme.

Sports and Recreation

186

Run a Marathon

You've been training for months, and the big race is finally here. For peak performance, heed the following suggestions.

Steps

1   Position yourself at the starting line according to your predicted pace.

2   Start slowly – this is the key to finishing in good form. Check your time at the 2-mile marker. If you're going faster than your target pace, then slow down.

3   Avoid attacking hills too aggressively. You'll need to conserve energy for the rest of the course.

4   Drink water or sports drinks at every rest station, even if you don't think you're thirsty.

5   Resist the urge to pick up your pace between miles 4 and 10; stay relaxed, calm and focused. Breathe rhythmically and pretend this is a practice run.

6   Towards the middle and end of the race, pour water over your head at each station, in addition to drinking it.

7   Carry power gels or other sports foods, or get them at rest stations if offered; eat what has worked for you in your practice runs.

8   Try to maintain your pace between mile 10 and mile 20 of the marathon. If you've gone through the first 10 miles too quickly, don't try to keep up your pace. A common error is to run too fast for the first 20 miles.

9   Shake out your arms and change your form for a few strides to provide relief between mile 14 and mile 20 of the race.

10 Draw willpower from the runners around you—concentrate on passing them or following one.

11 Slow down and visualise the finish if you hit the wall at mile 20. Think in terms of how much time is left, and approach the remaining distance as a 10-km race.

12 Gather your remaining strength for a final push during the last 2 miles; use the sight of the finish line and the crowd's cheers to overcome fatigue and discouragement.

13 Stay loose as you approach the finish. Keep your knees up and your arms moving. Run hard at least a dozen strides beyond the finish line, to keep yourself from slowing before you cross it.

14 Congratulate yourself—you deserve it!

✳ Tip

Understand that there's no shame in walking and no shame in dropping out if you can't continue. Listen to your body.

⚠ Warnings

Never attempt a marathon without proper training; this event is incredibly hard on the body. A good training programme will help prevent injury.

Do not attempt to run a marathon if you have sustained an injury during training.

187

Catch a Wave

The surf may be up, but you can't surf until you master this critical skill of catching and riding a wave.

◎ Steps

1 Paddle out beyond the breaking waves, sit on your board facing out to sea and wait for a good wave.

2 Sit just behind the middle of your board, with the nose pointing slightly out of the water, so you can easily pivot in any direction to paddle for a wave.

3 When you see a good wave coming, swing your legs up behind you to lie down on your board, and paddle to position yourself near the peak, where the wave is highest and will break first. If you are too far out,

Sports and Recreation

the wave won't be ready to break, and if you are too close to shore, the wave will immediately break and thrash you.

4. After paddling into position, sit up on your board and spin it around until you point in the direction you want to go when the wave picks you up.

5. Lie down when a choice wave swells your way. Paddle in the direction the wave is moving so that it overtakes you just before it breaks.

6. Note which way the wave is breaking: from your left to the right, for example. Eventually, you'll be propelled towards the beach and will want to surf sideways away from the break.

7. Accelerate your paddling as the wave approaches, applying full power as the wave picks you up and propels you.

8. Don't stop paddling until you feel the wave completely propelling you and your board. Keep your weight as far over the nose of the board as you can without dipping it under the water.

9. Grab the rails (edges) of your board directly beneath your shoulders and push up when you are sure the wave is taking you.

10. Quickly pop up from the rails of your board, pushing the board down into the face of the wave and quickly pulling your legs up beneath you.

11. Put your left foot forwards if you're regular-footed, or place your right foot forwards if you're a goofy-foot. Your feet should be roughly perpendicular on the board, depending on your own comfort. Keep in mind that the positioning of your feet depends on the size and shape of your board, but the position should enable you to instantly turn and control your board.

12. Lean to your wave-side rail (in this case, the right side). You should now be zipping along, riding the perfect wave.

❄ Tips

Keep your eyes focused down the wave, especially as you pop to your feet. The second you lean your weight back, you'll lose the wave.

Different breaks and different types of waves have different tendencies.

Take mental notes on each wave you miss and make corrections. Then try again.

Lay your board on the sand and practise pushing up and popping to your feet. When you pop up, try to plant your feet in the riding position, so you won't have to make adjustments as you drop in. Be careful not to break your fins or get sand in your wax, however.

⚠ **Warning**

Observe the rules of surfer right-of-way, allowing other surfers to catch the wave when appropriate. If you "drop in" (catch an already breaking wave) in front of another surfer, that person will, justifiably, get very angry with you.

188

Climb Mount Everest

Everest can mercilessly test even those who respect it. Whether you choose a packaged, guided expedition or trek with friends, there are several things to keep in mind.

◎ **Steps**

1   Start training today. Take mountaineering courses that teach you about technique, equipment, routes and survival. Then begin a minimum of two to three years of regular practice climbs in high alpine terrain, including steep faces, rough rocks, night climbs, ice falls and snow climbs.

2   Get a complete physical check-up. You'll need healthy veins and arteries to pump lots of blood to your brain and muscles, as well as to warm your body. Keep your blood pressure and cholesterol down.

3   Raise the cash. You'll need plenty—even a low-budget trip will cost around £35,000, with guided package trips soaring to double this. Realise that permits are expensive; then add travel, food, equipment, oxygen, insurance and Sherpa fees. Consider looking for sponsorship deals to cover your expenses.

4   Plan a May expedition. The weather is most cooperative then – when it isn't a whiteout, with 160 km/h (100 mph) winds blowing. Six months in advance, you'll need to file for permits from the Nepalese administration, sending copies of passports and climbing letters of recommendation for your team. You'll also need to contact a trekking agency to help you with transporting your gear and to contract Sherpas to aid you on your climb. For more information, contact the Nepalese Embassy in London, or the Nepal Mountaineering Association in Kathmandu, Nepal.

Sports and Recreation

5. Pack a first aid kit, medications, satellite phone, walkie-talkies, laptop computer, padlocks for bags, tents, sleeping bags, mountaineering clothing, climbing equipment and ropes, water, food, rubbish bags, sunscreen, vision protection, oxygen bottles and anything else you can fit on a yak or on your back, or that you can hire a Sherpa to carry for you. Make sure you've tested all your gear in cold, severe conditions before you pack it.

6. Get yourself to Kathmandu, Nepal, where your expedition truly begins. You can fly a number of international carriers connecting through major airports; none of these flights will be direct or nonstop. Jet lag is guaranteed. Check in with the local authorities, pay your fees and organise your crew.

7. Trek from Lukla to Base Camp at 5,400 m (17,500 ft). Scale the Khumbu Icefall up to 6,100 m (20,000 ft). Rest at Camp I in the Valley of Silence. Push on to Camp II at 6,500 m (21,300 ft). Scale the Lhotse Face and climb to Camp III at 7,400 m (24,000 ft). Rest and acclimatise for the trip to Camp IV, which at 8,000 m (26,000 ft) is the only camp located in the "death zone".

8. Charge the summit when you have a weather window. Start early in the morning, before sunrise, with extra down mittens and plenty of oxygen.

9. Sit atop the 8,850 m (29,035 ft) summit and know that you are at the highest point on earth. And mentally prepare for the descent – getting down is just as dangerous.

10. Pack out all of your empty oxygen bottles and rubbish to get back your environmental deposit and leave the mountain with good karma.

✳ Tips

Climb with people you know and trust, and who have extensive experience.

Ask other climbers who have tackled Everest to recommend the most skilled and reliable Sherpas.

Drink lots of purified water to stay hydrated.

⚠ Warnings

Stay warm, or risk losing body parts.

Climbing Mount Everest puts you at risk of severe injury, disease and possibly death from avalanche, falling rocks, crevasse falls, exhaustion, dehydration, frostbite, pneumonia, dysentery, Khumbu cough, whiteout disorientation, hypothermia, high-altitude cerebral and pulmonary œdema, and other hazards.

Be prepared to call off your summit attempt due to fatigue or poor weather conditions.

189

Use eHow

eHow.com is the website where you can find out how to do just about everything – and purchase the products and services you need to do it. Here's how to get the most from our site.

◎ Steps

1 Go online, type "www.ehow.com" in your browser's web-address field and press Enter or Return. Welcome to our home page!

2 Search for a how-to (what we call an "eHow") by typing a question – such as "How do I water a lawn?" – in the search field at the top of the page. Click "Do it" to search our database of eHows.

3 Or browse through our eHow centres, such as Home & Garden. You'll find these listed on our home page, and you can also find them via colour-coded navigation tabs that are visible on every page.

4 Read the eHow on the topic you've chosen. Note that some eHows also include video instructions.

5 As you're reading, check out tips contributed by other eHow users. (See "Ask Someone on a Date" or "Boil an Egg" for hundreds of enlightening examples.) If it's something you know how to do well, why not contribute your own tip?

6 Look for the handy shopping list that accompanies each eHow, and notice the featured books and tools. Just click on whatever you need to buy in order to get things done – or visit the eHow shop. The products you choose to buy travel with you in a virtual shopping cart as you go through the site.

7   Probe further into the eHow universe by clicking on Related eHows. Or explore other websites associated with your topic by clicking on one or more Related Sites.

8   Share favourite eHows with friends and family using our E-mail to a Friend feature. You can send any eHow – with a special message of your own – to anyone you want.

9   While you're online, sign up for our award-winning newsletter and be kept up to date on the latest eHow happenings.

10 Personalise your view of the eHow site by creating a My eHow page, for your favourite eHows, important reminders and any other goodies you choose to put there.

11 Put information in the palm of your hand by downloading any eHow to your personal device – for instant reference wherever you need it.

12 Take advantage of the time you've freed up by using our site to do the things you love. Or try something new and different: Start a business, paddle a canoe, win a sandcastle competition, plan a salsa party, redecorate your living room – or any of thousands of other things – using eHow's step-by-step instructions.

❋ Tips

If you don't have the time or desire to do a task, we can still assist you in getting the job done. Look for the Who Can Help You With This section to find people and services that can help you complete just about any task.

Check out our site regularly for new and timely features. For example, our seasonal centres come to life at holiday time to help you enjoy the festivities in new and creative ways. And the eHow shop will help make holiday shopping a breeze.

Share with us what you think of our site or this book. E-mail us directly at feedback@ehow.com.

⚠ Warning

eHow can be highly addictive. People come to our site to find out how to do one task and end up learning a lot of other things along the way. Visit eHow.com only if you're prepared to learn more – and do more – than you ever thought you could.

Index

Index

Index

Index

Index

Index